Hip Hop Dance

Recent Titles in
The American Dance Floor

Hip Hop Dance

Mohanalakshmi Rajakumar

The American Dance Floor

GREENWOOD

AN IMPRINT OF ABC-CLIO, LLC
Santa Barbara, California • Denver, Colorado • Oxford, England

Copyright 2012 by Mohanalakshmi Rajakumar

All rights reserved. No part of this publication may be reproduced, stored in a
retrieval system, or transmitted, in any form or by any means, electronic,
mechanical, photocopying, recording, or otherwise, except for the inclusion of
brief quotations in a review, without prior permission in writing from the
publisher.

Library of Congress Cataloging-in-Publication Data

Rajakumar, Mohanalakshmi.
  Hip hop dance / Mohanalakshmi Rajakumar.
    p. cm. — (The American dance floor)
  Includes bibliographical references and index.
    ISBN 978–0–313–37845–4 (hardback) — ISBN 978–0–313–37846–1 (ebook)
1. Hip-hop dance—United States. 2. Hip-hop dance—Social aspects. I. Title.
GV1796.H57R35   2012
793.3'1973—dc23   2011043293

ISBN: 978–0–313–37845–4
EISBN: 978–0–313–37846–1

16 15 14 13 12   1 2 3 4 5

This book is also available on the World Wide Web as an eBook.
Visit www.abc-clio.com for details.

Greenwood
An Imprint of ABC-CLIO, LLC

ABC-CLIO, LLC
130 Cremona Drive, P.O. Box 1911
Santa Barbara, California 93116-1911

This book is printed on acid-free paper ∞

Manufactured in the United States of America

Contents

Contents

Series Foreword

From the Lindy hop to hip hop, dance has helped define American life and culture. In good times and bad, people have turned to dance to escape their troubles, get out, and have a good time. From high school proms to weddings and other occasions, dance creates some of our most memorable personal moments. It is also big business, with schools, competitions, and dance halls bringing in people and their dollars each year. And as America has changed, so, too, has dance. The story of dance is very much the story of America. Dance routines are featured in movies, television, and videos; dance styles and techniques reflect shifting values and attitudes toward relationships; and dance performers and their costumes reveal changing thoughts about race, class, gender, and other topics. Written for students and general readers, The American Dance Floor series covers the history of social dancing in America.

Each volume in the series looks at a particular type of dance such as swing, disco, Latin, folk dancing, hip hop, ballroom, and country & western. Written in an engaging manner, each book tells the story of a particular dance form and places it in its historical, social, and cultural context. Thus each title helps the reader learn not only about a particular dance form, but also about social change. The volumes are fully documented, and each contains a bibliography of print and electronic resources for further reading.

Acknowledgments

Every book is the culmination of knowledge both on the part of the writer and researcher as well as all the others who were interested in finding out more about a similar topic. Hip hop is a complex cultural phenomenon that critics, scholars, and participants have been writing about for over 30 years. I am indebted to the large body of work, including books, films, and music, which has informed this book.

A special thanks to George Butler for his patience in working with ever-extending deadlines. Many thanks to Geoff Harkness for access to his *I Am Hip Hop* research archives.

I'm grateful to the Georgetown University-Qatar library, the premier research library in the country. Without its support and services I could not have had access to the materials needed to write this book. I also thank Fatima Mussa for leads on interviews and Jennifer Martens for her research assistance.

Lastly to the b-boys, b-girls, DJs, MCs, and graffiti artists who were there when it all began, thank you for sharing with us your creativity, energy, and drive which have created one the most vivid cultures of the twentieth century—hip hop.

And to those who are still at it, even now, all over the world: and ya' don't stop, ya'll.

Timeline

1948	Bronx Expressway construction begins, which causes the decline of the Bronx.
1971	Graffiti writer TAKI 183 begins leaving his tag all over New York City.
1973	DJ Kool Herc (Clive Campbell) DJs his first party with his sister.
1977	Break dancing group the Rock Steady Crew forms in the Bronx.
1977–1987	Often referred to as the era of "old school" hip hop (though there are many different opinions as to the exact dates for "old school").
1979	Sugar Hill Records releases first rap song, "Rapper's Delight."
1981	Articles appear in the *New York Times* and *Village Voice* about break dancing.
1982	Grandmaster Flash and the Furious Five release "The Message."
1983	*Flashdance* features cameos by Rock Steady Crew b-boys; break dancing is now a household word.
	Style Wars, first documentary on hip hop culture, is released.

1984   Russell Simmons and Rick Rubin establish one of the most important recording labels for the hip hop industry, Def Jam Records.

Mainstream movies about break dancing and hip hop culture, *Beat Street* and *Breakin'*, are released.

New York City Breakers and others perform at closing ceremonies of Los Angeles Olympics.

1987–1994   Often referred to as the "Golden Age of hip hop" (with varied opinions on the end, some as late as 1996).

1988   First issue of *The Source*, magazine on hip hop culture.

Premiere of *Yo! MTV Raps* television show.

N.W.A. releases *Straight Outta Compton*, establishing gangsta rap as a genre.

First year in which rap outsells any other type of music.

1999   Hip hop artist Lauryn Hill wins five Grammys, the most ever by a female artist.

Introduction: The Birth of the Hip Hop Nation

The birth of hip hop as a cultural movement which characterized music, dance, dress, and speech began in neighborhoods in the South Bronx, sometimes known as the "Boogie Down" borough of New York City. Boogie Down Bronx, as many came to refer to it, arose from the reputation of the Bronx as the source of musical mixing and innovation in the 1970s as sampling of funk and disco led to break dancing and rap, through the experimentation of teenagers living in the neighborhood. The development of hip hop into a global culturally, musically, and linguistically identifiable trend attests to its complex origin and appeal.

The term *hip hop* refers to the elements of this youth culture started in the multiethnic mix of the Bronx in the 1970s, including African American and Puerto Rican youth, as well as other Latinos and Afro-Caribbean immigrants. Thus hip hop was created as a cross-fertilization of diverse cultures for and by youth (Flores 138). Created by and for teenagers and people in their twenties to define what was "in," hip hop drew on the strength of related art forms including contemporary film, music, and cultural traditions for inspiration (Schloss, "Foundation" 4). Self expression, earning respect, and originality were key elements of hip hop culture which appealed to the otherwise socially and materially disenfranchised youth of New York City (Green 12). More or less a grassroots movement, hip hop and its elements were introduced to most DJs, MCs, and graffiti artists during their teenage years by friends.

Floor-to-ceiling exhibition of graffiti created by youngsters for a design class project at City College of New York in 1972. (AP Photo/Ron Frehm.)

As rapper MacAdam of the Chicago underground scene remembers:

> As for DJ-ing, to be completely honest, it was to keep me out of trouble. The s**t I was doing, it was kind of like well, let me find something a little bit more positive to do. And I had other friends that were involved. My best friends were part of the Chicago Tribe, like the whole party crew in Chicago. So I'd go to their house, and they would teach me how to DJ and I'd learn and eventually I just couldn't stop. . . . (Harkness, unpublished data)

If rap was the voice of hip hop, then graffiti became its public face and break dancing its physical embodiment (Fitzgerald 7). In a 30-year period, however, the commercial focus of hip hop would narrow to a musical genre largely identified with the experiences of the urban African American male. The ability of hip hop to simultaneously represent both its foundational elements from the 1970s as well as the development of the modern rap music industry is a testament to its complexity and importance in American culture. The range and complexity of hip hop culture is explained this way by rapper Alize of the Chicago underground scene: "The elements of hip hop is—everybody's got their different aspects—it's taggers, all different races, breakdancers is hip hop. Spray painting and everything, graffiti on the walls" (Harkness, unpublished data).

Ethan Brown characterizes the 1970s and the advent of hip hop as part of the "dance floor democracy" when anyone with creativity, energy, and style could take to the dance floor and win the respect of others. As the music became as integral to the movement as the dancing, there was a shift in perception and performance (Brown 89). When talking about hip hop dance and culture it is important to make a distinction between the origins of the movement, prior to the media attention and involvement (1970–1990), and after media exposure and interest from the recording industry.

The first phase, from the 1970s into the 1980s, was characterized by live, original interactions between dancers, graffiti artists, DJs, and MCs at street parties held in the Bronx. The second phase, beginning in the 1980s with the first popular rap singles played on the radio, was characterized by the consumption of recorded music by those who had no connection to its urban themes. Built on the traditions of existing music from jazz, blues, disco, and funk, hip hop music was a culmination of multiple cultural influences (Dyson and Daulatzai 4). This transition from hip hop as a series of connected, participatory activities into hip hop as a musical form for the consumer is one of the important enduring distinctions made by those who consider themselves "old school" with a view towards others as having sold out to consumerism (Schloss, "Making Beats" 33). Watching a contemporary tour of a rapper's mega-mansion on *MTV Cribs*, a show that takes viewers into the homes of famous artists, athletes, and actors, might raise questions about how far hip hop has come from its roots as a vehicle for the frustrated ambitions of a socioeconomically deprived generation (Heath, "Hip Hop" 715). Before piquing the interest of the recording industry, rap music began as the placement of rhythmic rhymes over the top of beats; both the words and the music were often chosen spontaneously during live performances. Both rap and hip hop were real-life experiences of youth in disadvantaged neighborhoods on the East Coast.

At the core of hip hop values is an investment in what Steven Hager defines as a "subculture that has created its own graphic art, dance, fashion, and musical styles" (x). The term *hip hop* was originally used to describe a style of music, dance, dress, and speech associated with the anti-institutional voice of rebellion which emerged in the Bronx

Kids dancing between 5th Ave and 52nd Street in New York City, 1984. (AP Photo/ Mario Cabrera.)

in the 1970s. It began as improvisational street dancing by American-born African Americans as well as first- and second-generation Latinos (Price 1). In the rawest sense, hip hop was an outlet for inner-city youth who were otherwise ignored by mainstream institutions including the government and schools. By the 1980s, hip hop culture and break dancing had spread to the suburbs across America, making it a nationwide phenomenon (Apell and Hemphill 386). In the decades following, it would spread around the world from Canada to Denmark. The four elements of hip hop culture are commonly defined as graffiti writing, break dancing, turntable spinning, and rapping (Grant 113). Critical to each of these various art forms is the creativity the individual brings to the particular craft.

Largely rooted in youth culture, break dancing and graffiti writing could be found on street corners, in public parks, and in subway stations (Watkins 9). Originally used by gangs to mark their territory or display their strength of membership, graffiti became a powerful tool for self-expression in the hands of individuals. Techniques in graffiti writing underwent a transition from black scrawled, spray-painted phrases in the 1960s to more elaborate and colorful designs with the

Graffiti in the New York City subway, 1972. (AP Photo.)

advent of hip hop culture. In the hands of some of the most creative forerunners, including PHASE 2 and TAKI 183, graffiti work or "tags" became eye-catching and original. By 1975, graffiti was the visual marker of the burgeoning culture. Graffiti "taggers" who left their personalized imprints on everything from subway cars to the sides of buildings also proliferated around this period as young people yearned for hopeful expressions of identity (Rahn 4). Working mostly at nighttime and by sneaking into the yards, or holding areas for the city's subway cars, graffiti writers became a challenge to the civil authorities.

Graffiti became a way of getting "published" for the tagger who may not have other educational or economic resources (Banes 14) to establish a presence in the public space as an artist. Taggers often renamed themselves with symbolic nicknames—a trend that would also be mimicked by DJs, MCs, and break dancers—and thrived in a close-knit community where people knew each other and respected a closely guarded commodity. Other similarities between graffiti tagging and break dancing include the terms used for identifying good work—"burning" the competition—or "battles," where dancers or taggers demonstrate their skills in order to establish a winner (Rahn 20). These artistic battles became a type of cultural warfare among teenagers who had few other means of inexpensive entertainment. In the case of graffiti, the desires to be the best or most prolific writer were often synonymous, and the subway trains, billboards, and other stationary objects in the urban landscape of New York became the canvas for the ambitious.

Almost by accident the work of taggers was discovered by two photojournalists in the 1980s. Martha Cooper and Harry Chalfant began photographing the work of graffiti artists as it appeared on subway cars in the New York City transit system. In Chalfant's Soho loft, people would leave messages on his answering machine of when and where to find freshly painted trains. The pair compiled their shots of the subway cars and shopped it around publishers in New York. The public opinion regarding subway writing, as it was first known, was divided over whether it was art or vandalism. The book was not picked up by any American publisher. Instead, finding interest overseas, it quickly became a classic, showcasing the range of creativity and talent used by subway writers on the trains that ran routes in the elevated parts of the subway in Brooklyn and the Bronx. Graffiti came into international circulation with the publication of *Subway Art* (Cooper and Chalfant 124). Both Cooper and Chalfant became hip hop photojournalists as well as producers of films and contributors to numerous books about graffiti, as well as b-boying.

In Chicago, Illinois, graffiti became a racially inclusive avenue for white teens wanting to participate in hip hop culture, as Visual, a rapper in the underground Chicago hip hop scene, explains:

> ... the funny thing is that here in Chicago, it was the graffiti scene that got a lot of the white kids involved and accepted. Because that's what they did and they were good at it and they were down. They were climbing ... running around and tagging on cop cars and punching other crews in the face. So they did the same [as] every other graf writer did, so it was like I don't give a s**t if you're white, black or what. You're down with my crew and that's how it went down. (Harkness, unpublished data)

Creativity, self-expression, and ability to define one's identity were important values shared by both graffiti artists and hip hop dancers.

In the early days of hip hop there was crossover between graffiti artists, DJs, and break dancers as someone interested in dance could also decorate a stage with graffiti for a DJ (Rose, "Black Noise" 35). In some cases where graffiti artists were also b-boys, a way to lay claim to a move you invented was to spray paint it as graffiti, thereby establishing it as yours both while dancing as well as via text in a public space. The combination of these activities resulted in a vibrant social street culture in contrast to the economically impoverished surroundings of the South Bronx in the 1970s and 1980s.

The rise of hip hop culture coincided with one of the most economically and socially depressed periods for the Bronx was well as the entire city. The signs of urban decay surrounded the youth of the day: the median household income in the Bronx was $5,200, the sale of heroin was rampant, police brutality was a documented fact of life, and the city of New York itself faced bankruptcy with a deficit of $7.3 million (Fricke and Ahearn vii). The advantages of such a loose social structure probably contributed to the atmosphere in which street parties were held with competitive speaker systems and block parties and gatherings in subway stations and outdoor parks were held on a regular basis.

The DJs would often illegally plug into the streetlamps and reroute other city-run electrical sources in order to power their sound systems. It was no accident that many of the early DJs were of West Indian descent; their powerful speakers and promotion of outdoor parties were reminiscent of Jamaican block parties with reggae music and the practice of "toasting" and "boasting" by the DJ over the music. In the Bronx, these young men, mostly in their 20s, created music by stitching together sounds from the songs of others, hosting parties outdoors or in gyms and community centers. As the instances of these parties grew, so did the promotion of them and the accompanying door charges. The money made by the fixers was the earliest instance of the ability of hip hop culture to generate revenue streams: the teenage organizers would often use the previous night's earnings to buy sneakers, new clothes, or better equipment for the next party.

The youth engaged in these activities were from African American, Latino, or Caribbean origins. Tagging, breaking, spinning, and MCing from 1965 to 1984, they became the original creators of the "Hip Hop generation." This era was generally acknowledged as the time when graffiti, breaking, spinning, and rapping originated in

New York and spread to the rest of the country as commercial activities (Patricia Collins 2). The diverse mix of clothing, music, and dance gave character to the movement we now know as hip hop. Retrospectively this can be referred to as the first generation of the hip hop movement (Saddik 125). Over a 35-year period, the distinctions would grow between hip hop as a creative culture and hip hop as a money-making enterprise.

The "hip" in the term *hip hop* came to define the growing subculture as something cool, and eventually *hip hop* itself came to refer to dance, music, dress, and even speech. The various strands that made up hip hop culture were drawn from a range of influences in the African American and Latino cultures. The tradition of oral poetry, for example, would have echoes in the rhyming lyrics created by MCs. The innovation and passion in dance used by b-boys and b-girls could be seen in step shows, double-dutch games, and martial arts movements (Schloss, "Foundation" 8).

The early days of breaking did include b-boys and b-girls, but as the media would gain interest in the performances, female dancers would become vastly outnumbered in crews and on television. The reasons for this were rooted not only in the masculine emphasis of hip hop culture but also in the social expectations of good behavior for girls as opposed to boys: breaking consisted of movements such as spinning on one's back, crotch grabbing, or other symbols of mostly male swagger that were not considered gender appropriate for young girls. Throughout the films and articles of this period, there are references to b-boys and b-girls, though in many instances the historical focus (1970s–1980s) is on b-boys, as they comprised the majority of the break dancing crews. This volume will explore the intersection of the various elements that comprise hip hop culture as well as focus on the development of the dance styles that came to define it and will also further examine the contributions of women as dancers, graffiti artists, and rappers.

Decline of the Bronx, Rise of Hip Hop

The socioeconomic decline of the Bronx began in 1955, and by the 1970s the borough was an economically devastated area, largely due to lack of funding and poor management of the city's finances; this, in addition to structural changes in the Bronx, physically and metaphorically changed the dynamics of the neighborhood. The construction of the Cross Bronx Expressway, which began in 1948, divided the neighborhood by allowing people to move into the suburbs and commute into the city, while those who couldn't afford the mortgages were left within the Bronx. In order to make room for the above-ground parts of the subway, the homes of hundreds of families were destroyed. The presence of the subway resulted in the migration of many small businesses and the affiliated middle-class owners who had previously lived there. White families and entrepreneurs fled to the suburbs to set up in large homes. In the city, the proliferation of tenement-style housing now called the projects or apartment blocks contributed to the impoverished urban landscape, which would soon be populated by rival gangs and associated street violence. The Bronx became synonymous with racial tensions as riots and looting broke out. Yet this same troubled neighborhood boasted a diverse make-up of youth from African Americans to Afro-Caribbean youth and Latinos. The diversity among the youth population would eventually fuel the development of hip hop culture into music, dance, film, dress, and television.

The visual markers of urban decay included the distinctive work of taggers, or graffiti artists who placed their unique names on subway cars and the sides of buildings (Starr and Waterman 376). Responding to their lack of access to adequate housing or after-school activities, break dancing and graffiti expressed the creative energies of the underprivileged youth population (Patricia Collins 191). Graffiti and break dancing allowed otherwise marginalized youth to come together in meaningful groups that were not centered on violence and to express their creativity and individuality in a positive community of their own creating. TAKI 183 (aka Demetrius, of which "Taki" is a derivative) is perhaps one of the most famous early graffiti artists, made so by a 1971 article in the *New York Times*, "Taki 183 Spawns Pen Pals," about his work all over the city (Price 187). Many credit him with sparking the popularity of tagging, as he was the earliest and most prolific tagger. The teenager left his signature or "tag" riding the subway during his day job as a messenger after being inspired by a fellow artist in his neighborhood. Beginning in the summer of 1970, TAKI 183 wrote on subways, walls, and parked vehicles with a wide marker as opposed to spray paint (Price 187).

Soon after there were many imitation graffiti artists using TAKI 183's style and similar names and numbers as nicknames (Rahn 4).

The response of the city to graffiti was to pull affected subway cars as soon as possible and have them chemically treated or wiped clean. As it became harder to leave tags on subway cars, taggers shifted to freight trains and moved from valuing frequency of tags to marking highly visible surfaces as the best taggers competed for space and prominence on city streets, buildings, and vehicles. Those who were able to cover the most ground held the most respect in the graffiti tagging community, and those who had few tags were given diminutive status as "scribbler" or "toys" as opposed to "writers" who could claim distinctive and recognizable styles. In the hierarchy of graffiti artists, the most talented taggers aspired to be writers. Often groups of taggers would assemble to produce a graffiti mural or larger piece of work (Rahn 7), but only after sketching it out in books or on paper. It was not uncommon for these designs and sketches to be passed around and critiqued by others before they were attempted in public.

The criteria for evaluating graffiti were as serious and established among the writers as those of any other art form: size, location, complexity of design, and the materials used were each a factor in the prestige associated with a particular mural or piece. The more technical skill required, the larger the piece, the more colors used, and the harder the placement, whether on trains, cars, or other objects, the more respect a tagger received.

Tags were considered the lowest status because they were the easiest to do and were generally small markings done by individuals on the inside of subway cars. In the form of rapidly written stylized letters, taggers often used markers and left their imprint in the same place on many cars. Sometimes one at a time, and often tied together in groups of two or more, markers were some of the cheapest and easiest-to-use supplies of a tagger. Yet this was still a way to establish oneself as "king of the insides" if you were able to mark every car in a particular subway line (Castleman 26). The next step up from tagging was to "throw up," or use bubble letters to decorate the outside of a subway car. Someone who had covered many surfaces in one area would have "bombed" it; *bombin'* was one of many slang terms used to refer to graffiti writing. A writer could "burn" a competitor by his or her style, scale, or design. What was generally agreed to be bad form, however, was to burn another writer by superimposing one's tag on work that was already finished.

From this level, the design demands only grew more complicated. "End to ends" were when two writers would cover an entire car with work from one end to the other; the whole car would be an expanded version of the end to end with artwork from the top to the bottom of the car (excluding the windows). In the mid 1970s two consecutive train cars were the most to have been completed by any one writer; most large projects required a group working together. In most cases this meant an experienced writer sketching out the overall design and others painting in the backdrop (Castleman 35). This was certainly true for a whole train, which was roughly 12 feet high and 50 feet long. One of the best-known whole-train projects was the Merry Christmas train in December 1977 featuring Santa Claus and a whole range of holiday-related imagery.

The New York Transit Authority responded to the work of graffiti writers by pulling and cleaning trains as quickly as they could in addition to instituting chain link fences and dog patrols near subway cars. In the mid 1970s, though, it was a particularly difficult task to change popular attitudes or discourage teenagers from taking the risks to paint cars given the rise in interest and popularity of graffiti. The visibility of the tag gave the tagger legitimacy that the act of defacing public property otherwise denied them: "getting up," as it became known, was just as important as the quality of the work itself. The risk of getting caught by authorities only added to the daring and prestige of the larger murals. In New York at the time, when people were generally turned inward to their own situations or problems, subway art caused them to look outward at the world around them. Often the graffiti artists would hang around to watch the reactions of passengers as the cars they had painted were passing by (Castleman 20). Those who were able to establish a design and easily manipulate a spray can were often the most admired.

Graffiti writing is still in practice today, as one modern-day tagger, EAX (aka Angel Loayza) comments: "Graffiti nowadays has become the cool thing for marketing, commercials. . . . I used to always think about starting a graffiti marketing company, but now it's all over the place, for example TV, billboards, train ads" (Loayza). EAX has experienced the trajectory of graffiti in the popular culture, first as a semicrime accomplished by vandals:

> I become involved in graff back when I was in 7th grade . . . at that point it
> was really hard to get spray cans because there were no Home Depots.
> We only had small hardware stores where you needed to have

identification to prove that you at least 18 years or older. So we ended up always having to steal the spray paint. I became more and more interested in it when it felt like I was living a double life. (Loayza)

This double life is reminiscent of taggers admiring their work alongside strangers or passersby on bridges and at train stations. The contrast between the anonymity of the tagger's real identity and the hyper visibility of the tagged object, such as a subway train, contributed to feeling of accomplishment. EAX describes the pride in having his tag noticed:

Kind of like Spiderman I was known for my real name (Angel) and also for my tag (EAX). The more tags I had out on the street the more I became known. It became like a drug. I always remember how proud I felt when I met a famous graff artist and they asked me what my tag was . . . when I told them my tag they would say "oh I've seen that up" . . . it was the best feeling ever. . . . (Loayza)

EAX is not the only tagger to have gotten a young start with spray cans; SMURF (aka Marco Antonio) also began tagging in his early preteen years—at 11 years old—almost by accident, as he describes it: "One day I found a can of spray paint and went and put up Smurf in the swimming bath car park and numerous other places" (Antonio). SMURF's tag came from a nickname his cousins gave him as part of their CB radio nicknames, or handles. SMURF is still involved in the graffiti scene through training younger aspiring taggers and once in a while putting up a piece himself. His love of graffiti as art is apparent when he talks about the creative expression it allows artists:

True graffiti is true freedom, freedom to express one's self, be it a quick tag or an elaborate wildstyle burner. There are not many movements that can claim to be free of conformity. Graffiti has a young history, always evolving. It has taught me, by being creative respect, honor and discipline and I try to instill these important morals in the work I do with young people. (Antonio)

SMURF's love of graffiti speaks to its resonance for taggers in the 1980s and also today. In his opinion what makes a good piece is not subjective but can be somewhat defined: "A good piece has GOOD use of color, connections, 3d, background, characters, concept, fill in, use of space . . . but above all of this the piece has to flow and have movement. A good piece of graffiti could also be a nice tag with a good handstyle" (Antonio). Being able to recognize original pieces from those used by commercial entities is part of what EAX, SMURF, and other contemporary taggers feel is important to hold on to from the roots of early graffiti. In many instances DJs, b-boys, and MCs first were introduced to hip hop culture through graffiti. Often seen as a sign of urban blight, graffiti in the Bronx in the 1970s and 1980s was a form of unrestricted creative youth expression, and it is still used by many. Like many of the other elements of hip hop, graffiti spread to youth around the world, including cities such as Berlin, Germany. As one German tagger puts it: "A city without graffiti is a people without youth" (Henning).

Coinciding with this economic downturn were Black Power movements, which organized youth and middle-aged African Americans towards expressing their political and social consciousness in a collective identity. The Black Panthers, Nation of Islam, Young Lords, and Revolutionary Action Movement were all groups active in the 1970s with roots from the 1960s as an outgrowth of disenchantment with the 1950s nonviolent civil rights movement political dimensions; they competed for participation from teenagers with local school gangs, which were racially divided. For the youth of the South Bronx, however, these movements often seemed far removed from the realities of their everyday lives.

Not surprisingly, in this gap of self-expression, hip hop culture emerged as an alternative to the menace of gang-owned streets and acts of retaliation, and hip hop parties became safe places for youth to gather to participate in or watch competitive dancing, which featured the excitement, theatricality, and competitiveness of gang rivalry without the violence (Price 32). Some of the earliest contests were held in community centers, such as St. Martin's Church on 182nd Street and Cortona Avenue (Hagar 83).

Coming at a time when gangs and gang culture thrived, the roots of hip hop borrowed from the territorial nature and competitive nature of rival groups already present in the neighborhoods. Graffiti artists left their mark on specific areas as a way to distinguish themselves from the work of others, and also as a way of marking their place in certain neighborhoods or on specific train routes in a way similar to gangs establishing territories. DJs had loyal followers who would attend their parties exclusively and protect their equipment. MCs would engage in battles against one another to establish whose rhymes and lyrics were the most fluid or creative. One of the recurrent themes of hip hop culture across the four major elements was the test of one's skills against an opponent in a competitive, audience-observed setting. This type of dynamic interaction allowed youth to create reputations and names for themselves that were otherwise not possible in their resource-deprived environment. In order to establish yourself as a breaker, writer, DJ, or MC, you had to work for the title and then the recognition of your peers. Many DJs and MCs got their introduction to hip hop culture through tagging and graffiti.

Strive Tek remembers his own induction as a teenager into hip hop culture: "Back in that day, I used to be a tagger. More on like the art sense of hip hop in a way, with me and my boys back in high school. We used to go bombing and doing all sorts of graf" (Harkness).

DJs emerged as community leaders, having the same immigrant or first-generation origins as the taggers and dancers of early hip hop. Early DJs such as Afrika Bambaataa (aka Kevin Donovan) became cultural icons and role models who supplanted gang violence with dance competitions (Ogbar, "Hip Hop Revolution" 3). Commonly referred to as the Godfather of Hip Hop, Bambaataa was popular in the Bronx River East, and under his influence in the early 1970s, as well as that of other DJs, youth began affiliating with crews as expressions of local identity instead of with gangs. The crews mimicked the familial ties between gang members and their biological families. Often the older members of a crew would mentor those who wanted to learn the basics of b-boying until the new member could battle for his or her acceptance. Typically a crew would have six to 10 members at any one time, though this number could grow depending on its popularity.

Formerly a high ranking member of the Black Spades, an active African American gang of the South Bronx, Bambaataa, or "Bam," as he was also known, established a series of groups to draw youth to positive, peaceful activities. The Black Spades were one of many gangs that terrorized citizens living in the South Bronx, having begun in the late 1960s with a handful of members as the Savage Seven, and growing into the hundreds (Tokaji 100). The overall gang numbers in the Bronx were rising at the start of the 1970s: by some reports there were as many as 11,000 youth in gangs (Tokaji 100). The tensions between rival groups only increased when the city introduced busing into the

Afrika Bambaataa. (AP Photo/Henny Ray Abrams.)

school system as kids from the Bronx were sent to schools in Manhattan and vice versa.

Bambaataa's transition from gang leader to promoter of hip hop parties helped defuse the gang culture often rampant in night clubs as members who used to harass night-time revelers became competitors in the emerging hip hop dance and music scene as DJs, MCs, and b-boys. As Afrika Bambaataa, he was a central figure in the early development of hip hop culture as well as the use of dance as an authentic cultural expression. In 1973, what started as the Bronx River Organization would become the "Organization"; later it would be known as the Universal Zulu Nation, named after the precolonial empire in Africa and its king, Shaka Zulu, and it would bring together DJs, MCs, taggers, and break dancers (Ogbar, "Hip Hop Revolution" 3). In addition to being a pioneer of various aspects of hip hop culture, Bambaataa was an early promoter of political consciousness in hip hop as a means to address the social, economic, and political situation of nonwhite people against the mainstream. In the 1980s when the Zulu Nation spread to France and established the first of a series of new international networks, hip hop's future as a refuge for youth was evident (Alim 269).

Bambaataa was one of the first to consider the dancers at his parties as a cohesive group; he saw the potential in the youth looking for a good time to harness their energy as their own nation in spite of how others might define them (Wheeler 195). He would later add knowledge along with DJing, MCing, graffiti, and breaking as the fifth critical element to hip hop and encourage people to adhere to its socially conscious roots after discovery by the mainstream media. He was known to pick sections from unlikely party songs and tell partygoers after the fact that they had danced to the Monkeys or another song or group that they otherwise professed to hate (Schloss, "Making Beats" 32). In so doing he made people reconsider tracks and styles they had previously dismissed as uninteresting or unhip.

Bambaataa began taking his street parties around the community to gyms and community centers, gathering youth together who had previously turned to gangs for companionship and belonging. Notably, five of his b-boys were among the first members of what he called the Zulu Kings; the members of this group were some of the earliest to choose dance over violence (Ogbar, "Hip Hop Revolution" 3). The group fused dancers, graffiti artists, MCs, and DJs who wanted alternatives to the violence in the Bronx in the mid 1970s. The Zulu Kings were part of the first and earliest wave of b-boys (Fitzgerald 69–77).

Predominately made up of youth from the African American or Latino communities, crews were vital means of social expression. These crews functioned as informal social groups from a specific block; also known as posses, these groups quickly became features of the urban landscape, performing at neighborhood block parties, dances held in gyms, community centers, and parks (Starr and Waterman 377). Dancing became a hobby that was practiced all night. Fierce competitions came to define these events; their leaders encouraged dance competitions between members of the various crews and posses as acceptable means of establishing a group's reputation.

Winning these competitions became another way of dueling between rival gangs. Rivalries between crews, as groups of dancers came to be known, were handled in "battles," or competitions between groups from various neighborhoods across New York City. The battles became a foundational element of hip hop as the competitive element replaced gang violence with an emphasis on talent, expressiveness, and strategic moves as battle tactics (Schloss, "Foundation" 10–11). The battles were typically executed in six steps of dancers from the alternating crews, moving in a circle through a range of movements (Schloss, "Foundation" 88). The demand was for each group to directly respond to the others moves, with stamina and agility featuring prominently as important performance characteristics since most battles happened outdoors on sidewalks and in parks.

Crews in Brooklyn battled those in Uptown and challenges from the Bronx were issued against groups in Brooklyn (Cobb 3). These battles became a means of challenging the competitive instinct in a nonviolent and creative manner as the invention of new moves by crew members created more reasons to perform and compete against rivals (Tanz 48). Hip hop dance, and in particular break dancing, provided the means for creative expression as well as a nonviolent arena to contest the constantly shifting hierarchy of the Bronx's many gangs.

In the early days of hip hop several key figures influenced the music and therefore the dance styles. These included DJs and MCs whose parties gathered large crowds that then needed to be entertained. The hip hop movement rejected mainstream dance music and gained promoters in the form of DJs who were tired of playing the same disco music that appealed largely to white audiences. Mixing became a way for the DJ to create interruptions in the music, thereby creating a new track with the integration of two existing songs (Green 13). The energy and enthusiasm of dancers at parties were given a boost by the emergence of masters of ceremonies, or emcees, who came to be known in the hip hop world as MCs.

The threat of a fight was not uncommon, and so the DJ and MC would call out to the dancers to keep them engaged in the beat. This type of call to the dance floor and response was common in the African American tradition of live call-and-response and was one of the earliest developments in hip hop music (Wheeler 194). The functions provided by an MC replicated the social storytelling of a *griot*, or oral historian/poet/bard common in West Africa. The similarities between the griot and the MC included the ability to improvise and entertain and were dependent on their listeners. The rhymed storytelling of the *griot* and the MC would provide the essence of rap music, which would become one of the defining products of hip hop culture (Saddik 125). It was the MCs who kept the dancers moving late into the night as the dancers responded to the tracks being played. These

MCs were the first rappers, but it would be nearly a decade before DJs or MCs would realize they could record their freestyle work at street dances for commercial benefit (Rahn 2).

In the late 1970s, the freelance DJ with his portable sound system and records became a folk hero in the melting pot of the Bronx (Hagar 33). "Toasting," or speaking and rhyming to keep the crowd engaged, were the earliest precursors to MCing (Rivera 56). As the DJ created "music collages" by spinning together the beats of various records, the MC worked the crowd with freestyle rhymes which would eventually become rap music (Hemphill 386). Early party-hyping slogans such as "Ya rock and ya don't stop" or "to the beat ya'll" were used by MCs to keep the dancers moving and would eventually become standard hip hop phrases (Nelson 17). These were the earliest form of conversational rap, and MCs utilized these unrehearsed chants and repeated phrases throughout the course of the evening at will (Dimitriadis 183). Eventually these techniques would become more professionalized into the defining element of modern hip hop culture: the genre of rap music.

The combined effect of the DJ and MC was that of being at a live performance where the music adapted to the dancers at a particular venue. Recording these live performances in the form of mix tapes showed early on the economic value of hip hop music (Patricia Collins 13). In the 1970s, these dancers were mostly African Americans as well as first- and second-generation U.S.-born Latinos, but within a few decades the entire nation would experience the hip hop phenomena. Another major shift would be the rising popularity and commercial success of female artists. Originally characterized as a largely male cultural manifestation, hip hop would come to also celebrate the talents of female artists and dancers (Rivera 37). What no one could foresee was that this spontaneous youth creative expression that began in the recreational centers and on the streets of the South Bronx of New York City on the East Coast of the United States would develop into a international industry that included recording artists, music labels, and the advent of rap music as the defining feature of a movement with complex and diverse urban roots (Schloss, "Making Beats" 5).

From the 1990s onward, hip hop was characterized almost exclusively by a commercialized African American aesthetic very different from its polyethnic roots. Ironically, this underground genre of music, dance, dress, and speech would become one of America's most well-defined global exports (Heath, "Hip Hop Now" 715). The diverse range of definitions which the term *hip hop* evokes is an indication of its enduring importance to the contemporary American dance, musical, and social milieu. Simultaneously a culture and a genre of music, and also used to refer to a generation of youth at a particular moment in history, hip hop is a multifaceted social phenomenon worth investigating.

1

The "Breaks" in Break Dancing

The connection between hip hop music and dance was central to the development of rap music as well as break dancing. Both were outcomes of spontaneous live performances by DJs, MCs, and break dancers at community dances and competitions all over the Bronx and other parts of New York City in the 1970s. The intertwined nature of the DJs and MCs trying to keep the dancers moving on the dance floor with innovations in music as well as the efforts of the dancers themselves to "one up" each other contributed to flexible and organic creativity (Dimitriadis 181). The ability of a b-boy to make meaning in the performance circle, often spontaneously and with the support of onlookers, shared many similarities to the spinning of tracks by DJs and the rhythmic party chants of MCs, which were also highly improvisational and designed to impress the audience.

"Breaking" or break dancing, as it came to be called, was a form of improvised dance that began with an emphasis on the dancer or b-boy's individual style and flair. Requiring skill, athleticism, and hours of practice, b-boying became a way of staying out of trouble, developing a positive identity as well as a group of supportive peers, yet still staying on the streets for unconventional reasons. The teenage body performing dance became a means of self-expression similar to one achieved previously through the voice and singing (LaBoskey 112). Competition, domination, sexuality, and reputation building were all aspects of life as a b-boy; breaking reflected the cultural diversity of

1

Children break dancing after riots in Lawrence, Massachusetts. (AP Photo/Sean Kardon.)

the youth who resided in the Bronx, with differences between the styles of Puerto Rican and African American youth.

The energy of the dancer drove the sequence of steps and moves executed in the performing circle. B-boys strove to give the impression of jointlessness and fluidity, to represent self-confidence, and to win the title of the best. An ambitious teenage boy with hours to practice and perfect his claim could win a title or recognition in these competitions without much in the way of material resources. Taunts and boasts were popular to dig at one's opponent; they were embodied in physical movement, also called "razzing" (Banes 145). These dances would come to replace the physical gang warfare that had been prevalent in the neighborhood prior to the popularity of breaking—though the impulse to settle disputes with violence was often still an option.

The emphasis in the early days of breaking was on the style of footwork, called toprock, as well as the transitions into freezes or drops. Toprock and uprock, horizontal steps which open up the stance, were performed while standing, were designed to humiliate, and featured freestyling as well as spins and turns (Morgan, "Real Hip Hop" 209). The faceoff between dancers, and eventually their crews or groups, were battles for pride and ego among macho teenagers. Breaking was generally preformed in a circle and watched by other dancers cheering or watching the person in the middle. Later, as Latino youth became interested in breaking, the repertoire of the b-boy expanded to include acrobatic and pantomimed movements including spins as well as flips, as dancers circled each other, moving from upright to dancing on the ground (Banes 13). Critic Sally Banes separates break dancing into two periods: one largely characterized by amateurs, prior to exposure by the media, and the second performed by professionals after garnering commercial and media attention.

In the first period, that of the amateurs, break dancing was largely an "urban vernacular dance" or something used by African American and Puerto Rican youth in the Bronx as a way to demonstrate their athleticism in lieu of fighting. Breaking was a socially significant way to show one's skills and talents. As it grew in popularity and crews began to be featured in movies as well as on television, break dancing, and hip hop culture in general, was mined for its ability to sell records. Eventually the four original elements, DJing, MCing, graffiti writing, and breaking, would be augmented by dress and language. The audience for the movement grew from the neighborhoods of New York City to the country at large, and eventually the international market.

Early break dancing movements had roots in a variety of unexpected genres including the Brazilian martial art *capoeira*, jazz music, and martial arts. In jazz, for example, the improvised bridge of a song could be considered a "break" or a riff, much like what the b-boy or b-girl exhibited during the repeated breaks created by the DJ. In the Afro-Caribbean tradition familiar to many of the Latino youth native to the Bronx, the spontaneous and unbridled drumming and dancing that occurred at the height of voodoo rituals was similar to a break dancer "going off" (Banes 17).

The immediacy of the b-boy or b-girl doing a routine on the dance floor was one aspect of breaking essential to those experiencing it in person. The immediacy of the invented movements, and soon the music that came to accompany them, were thought to be so time sensitive that many of the early b-boys, DJs, and MCs had a difficult time imagining how it could ever be recorded. Parties were known to go on for hours, often without start or end times; DJs sampled the records of others in order to create their unique mixes, which often infringed on copyright; MCs were under pressure to keep the crowd moving and would use spontaneous lyrics rarely rehearsed beforehand or written down. In all senses hip hop and breaking depended on the energy of those present and their spontaneity in order to preserve its relevance to its participants.

Other influences on breaking included the diverse roots of the immigrants who populated the Bronx and other parts of New York in the 1970s. *Capoeira*, the Brazilian martial art, for example, emphasized the acrobatic flexibility of the dancers as well as dances from the Afro-Caribbean, African American, and Latino communities. Footwork, head-spins, backspins, and head movements were various moves used by break dancers during "battles," formal and informal dance competitions, or "breaks" against each other (Cobb 7; Hagar 83). Extended breaks, known as "freezes," were poses designed to be held for long periods. Freezes were practiced with an eye towards awing the crowd and outlasting the competitor's best move (Tanz 48). Often the freeze came at the end of a b-boy's turn in the circle, after which he would exit, having left a strong impression of strength and flexibility. Popular freezes could also have sexual overtones such as "the hump" where the dancer paused with his pelvis in the air, or rear end facing his opponent. The next dancer would often wait for the freeze before entering the circle to begin his or her turn. Humor and difficulty were the two elements critical to a good freeze (Banes 124). The popularity of the freeze is still evident in its usage by pop icons such as Justin Timberlake.

Credited with inviting the move "the suicide," a move related to the freeze, Frosty Freeze was the first to drop onto his back suddenly from being upright. The transitions into the suicide could vary from front flips to handsprings, headstands, or back flips. The drop gave the impression of being out of control and lying prone on the floor, while the freeze was characterized by a more deliberate and precisely held movement.

Competing for showmanship and respect, the b-girls and b-boys flooded the dance floors (Huntington 87). At the center of all hip hop dance is the b-boy and the b-girl; the dancers and the moves they take to the floor to bring the music alive with their bodies. Performed largely in community centers or outdoor parks in New York City in the 1970s, dances became a space shared by youth from a variety of backgrounds including African American and Latino. The most popular DJs in the Bronx at this time, Afrika Bambaataa, Kool Herc, Grandmaster Flash, and Mean Gene, were also some of the early pioneers in mixing techniques that further supported the development of break dancing. DJs generally had their area of the Bronx in which they played parties and pioneered their own techniques.

One of the earliest DJs was Kool Herc (aka Clive Campbell), whose territory was the West Bronx. Originally from Jamaica, and moving to the Bronx in 1967, he is the first person credited with using two record turntables to create smooth transitions between albums, arguably one of the first steps towards the development of the music which inspired b-boying. Nicknamed "Hercules" for his athletic frame, his introduction into hip hop culture began as a graffiti artist. His tag, Kool Herc, he would take with him into life as a DJ (Price 164–165). Herc, as he was also known, was an example of crossover in the early days of hip hop; DJs or MCs often began in the scene with other parts of hip hop culture such as graffiti art or b-boying. Unlike other DJs, Herc didn't play songs continuously; he instead created his own rhythms by picking out the best beats across a variety of records and playing these minute-long segments back to back (Tokaji 102).

Kool Herc played the beats in the popular funk music, reportedly removing labels from the records he used at parties to keep his choices secret from other DJs as well as to focus on isolating the sounds of various segments and not artists themselves (Hagar 33). The emphasis on the beat was counter to the disco music which was popular at the time, where the beat was often hidden within the melody. Kool Herc stripped away the melody and words of a song, isolating just the beats which he noticed dancers were waiting for before showcasing their favorite moves (Chang, "Can't Stop" 6). Parts of James Brown songs, the drum segments on Rolling Stones records, these were all fair game in the new world of spinning, scratching, and cutting (Rivera 56). Brown's hit "Get on the Good Foot" was one of the songs that would inspire a whole spinoff genre of music and dance. When Brown danced to his song on television, the swift footwork of his hustle is what many ascribe as an early inspiration to break dancers as the moves were repeated in clubs and at parties by enthusiastic dancers (Tokaji 102). Known as the Godfather of Soul, his spins, quick shuffles, knee drops, and splits demonstrated the energy and spontaneity break dancers would use as core values to b-boying (Fitzgerald 8).

DJ Kool Herc, a Jamican-born DJ whom many consider the father of hip hop.
(AP Photo/Bebeto Matthews.)

This discovery of reveling in the break and the corresponding influence on the dancers, which Herc attributes to noticing while standing
around during cigarette breaks while DJing, would revolutionize both
hip hop music and dance. Herc was also one of the earliest DJs to
"freelance talk" in order to keep the crowd moving during songs; a
technique that would later be picked up by MCs and then rappers
(Bradley 57).

The downbeat in a song, or when the rhythmic beats were played
alone, apart from the melody, highlighting the sound of only the beat
during a piece of music, was when the dance floor was likely to be
most frenzied as dancers were known to go wild (Schloss, "Making
Beats" 30). Herc is credited as the one who began to isolate these beats
and emphasize them in order to encourage the crowd to keep dancing
at its most energetic pace. The isolation of sounds from existing
records or the sampling of beats from the music of other artists kept

DJs from thinking of themselves as musicians. Instead they would utilize the beats in any genre from reggae to Latino funk music, even using beats from songs that were otherwise unpopular except for the core rhythms (Schloss, "Making Beats" 31). Though some saw sampling as stealing the work of others, sampling was also seen as a guerrilla move to reuse the beats of a song in the new context of the urban dance floor (Cheney 9).

The DJs' equivalents of musical instruments were directly linked to technological developments in music—the turntable, the record, and the microphone (Black Dot xv). Two turntables allowed Kool Herc to isolate the breaks in music, mix them together, and replay them continuously on a loop, or the "break beat" (Price 165). This allowed the DJ to extend the break in the song for as long as he wanted; continuously repeating the break, or a string of breaks, in effect created a new song (Chang, "Keeping It Real" 550). Soon two turntables, a mixer, and multiple copies of records with good beats were the staple for any DJ trying to build a reputation among party goers in the Bronx. Kool Herc was one of the earliest to establish a following in the Westside; his "Herculords" were twin speakers and an amplifier that allowed him to establish his own brand of music and DJ personality at parties held at 1520 Sedgwick Avenue, the main artery running through the Bronx, which were co-hosted and planned by his sister in the 1970s (Hagar 33). This technique was also used with funk music and salsa to highlight the beat of various songs without the melody for endless replays, but Kool Herc is one of the first credited with bringing it to break dancers. Originally hosting house parties in apartments, Herc's popularity grew to the point that he branched out into recreational centers and other community spaces. For some the price of the turntables was considerable, so they made do with "pause tapes," achieving the same looping of beat via a boom box, tape deck, and the pause button to smooth out the transition between the breaks. The pause button was better than the stop button, which came with a clicking sound, sure to interrupt the flow of the beat and to be noticed by the dancers (Caz xvi).

Kool Herc used two copies of the same record to play the break over and over between the two discs. One was used for backspin, turning clockwise, while the other played continuously, allowing him to play the break in the music repeatedly between the two discs, leaving out the melody but preserving the beat (Starr and Waterman 377). Kool Herc was also known to repeat words in time with the music in order to encourage the dancers to keep moving. This was considered the earliest form of rapping. In 1969, DJ Kool Herc is credited with coining the term *b-boy* for someone who was "breaking loose on the dance floor" as he would encourage dancers by shouting "b-boys go down" into the musical breaks (Green 25).

But the term itself was used in a variety of ways, including the way dancers would appear to lose all control at the height of the music, or the breaks in the song which were considered the best moments to dance to (Holman 36). Others also ascribe the term to street slang used at the time to describe someone who had temporarily lost control or was behaving irrationally; "going berserk," "going off," "went off" were all synonyms used in relation to the idea of breaking—both in real life and in dancing. Being able to release this kind of potent energy on the dance floor as opposed to real-life situations transferred much of the energy and angst of b-boys from gangs and other more violent activities. Eventually the lifestyle of a b-boy—strenuous practice for hours a day with the demands of acrobatic and gymnastic moves as well as competing by night—meant that crews had alternate means of settling differences as well as using their energies. Prior to the b-boy battles for recognition, clubs were invaded by gangs and their struggles for power. With the advent of hip hop parties where dancers and crews demanded respect by showcasing their skills, gangs held less prominence in the social arena.

Teenagers embraced this transition from street violence to street dance, but to the adults around them the effects were the same: boys as young as eight to 10 loitering in groups in the subway or on the street corner, posturing against rivals. One example of the early confusion between breaking and fighting is the story of the arrest of the High Times crew by police for fighting in the subway in Washington Heights. At the station the b-boys tried to explain that they weren't in fact starting a riot (as they had been accused) but having a dance off. The skeptical cops asked for proof, and they were surprised when the boys produced a list of moves, much like any dance troupe, that any one of them could perform but with odd names such as "the baby." Calling their bluff, the officers asked each one to come forward and perform. And they each did, getting them off the hook (Banes 126). But attitudes towards hip hop culture were not always positive.

Bobby Lovelock from Chicago remembers when graffiti and break dancing did not enjoy status as high art forms:

> A lot of graf artists couldn't write cause they got racked. For what? Throwin' up art on a wall. They got treated like they raped somebody, like they was threatening to kill somebody. . . . I mean through the eighties, not only was graffiti illegal but so was break dancing. They shut it down. If you was breaking on the corner in Chicago in 87, CPD [Chicago Police Department] would arrest you. Take you away for just breakin'. Now, you break, there's gonna be a crowd of people gathered around. People going ooh and tryin' to break they money out. (Harkness)

The characteristic elements of a good b-boy were athleticism, flexibility, and the endurance required to maintain sudden bursts of energy during the breaks as the dancers were evaluated by their audience (and judges during formal competitions) on their ability to convey a sense of attitude, originality, and perseverance throughout a song. These elements combined to convey a dancer's unique style and personality. While a b-boy could learn a series of moves, how he personalized them with his own flair underscored his talent as a persona. Generally executed in a circle with a return to the center of gravity, the b-boy or b-girl would use the center as a launching point for other moves and a placeholder to return to throughout his or her sequence (Schloss, "Foundation" 88). Handsprings or other aerial movements were also admired, in addition to head spins.

Many b-boys named themselves after a particular dance move that became their specialty, including flips, glides, or freezes (Banes 18). Nicknames were also popular for DJs and MCs as a way of defining the specific talent or characteristic central to their hip hop identities (Rose, "Black Noise" 36). Battles between MCs to prove who had the best rhymes, like the infamous one between Busy Bee (aka David Parker) and Kool Moe Dee (aka Mohandes Dewese), were also popular in the early 1980s in addition to those taking place between b-boys and their crews. These battles featured competition between MCs that would seem innocent and playful in comparison to the bitter rivalries that would rise up between rappers in the decades to come. The MCs' verbal dexterity was equivalent to the b-boy's physical flexibility.

Marcyliena Morgan explains the importance of rap lyrics to the expressive nature of hip hop culture: "Hiphop is not only concerned with the manifestation of words, discourse, and grammar but also the significance of those elements when used by a particular people, at particular times, in reference to particular events and for particular audiences" (191). Morgan's work with the underground rap community in LA informs her commentary and further highlights the importance of local and live performances for MCs. Wes Restless, a rapper in the Chicago hip hop scene, agrees with Morgan on the importance of the words used by the MC and his or her ability to manipulate language to surprise the listener: "First and foremost is rhythm and delivery. Cause if you're not saying it in a cool way, people aren't even gonna listen to your words. That and a knack for language. From there, vocabulary is pretty important—you have to be able to explain yourself and not say the same shit all the time" (Harkness).

Kool Herc, Afrika Bambaataa, and Grandmaster Flash were all DJs who helped shape the techniques of hip hop DJs. Reminiscent of the turf culture protected by gangs and their members, each DJ had a following established in a separate part of the Bronx, with Kool Herc playing to crowds on the Westside, Afrika Bambaataa near the Bronx River, and Grandmaster Flash from 138th Street to Gun Hill (Forman 68). These territories inspired vigorous debate among those who lived in them and attended the parties as to which DJ skills were the most important—the speed of Flash, or the eclectic mixing of Kool Herc—in short, who was the best DJ. The spirit of competition and creativity would be mimicked by the dancers for whose enjoyment the DJs would work so hard. The lines between graffiti, DJs, MCs, and break dancers were not distinct during this period. As Gustav Mandible remembers, they were very blurred, and it was quite easy to mix across the four foundational elements:

> Me, I've been involved all my life. My cousin was into break dancing and DJ-ing. He's way older than I was. So ever since I was little, I was involved into all that stuff. We would go to [a club] and I'd be break dancing, I'd be the youngest one break dancing. He got me into tagging, so I've always been involved. I started writing when I got into high school with these guys. Most of the time, I wanted to DJ but I didn't have the equipment. (Harkness)

Here again is a reference to a preteen staying out of trouble, hanging out with his cousin, and encountering all of the four elements of hip hop culture. His exposure to being a DJ was almost an afterthought to his roles as b-boy and graffiti tagger. But the reaction to the music by b-boys and b-girls, the local dancers, is what encouraged DJs to find the next beat and promoted a competition among DJs themselves to keep the crowds moving (Price 1). The interaction between the dancers and those playing the music became one of the earliest developments of the hip hop scene as DJs experimented with various techniques in order to keep the parties going well into the night. This isolating of the breaks in music and mixing them came to be known as "break-beat" music and directly led to the advent of break dancing, which was a departure from the group dancing at disco clubs in the 1970s. While slam and punk dancing were also for individuals, neither the musical style nor the style of dance appealed to those who embraced break dancing. Dancers who moved without partners came to be known as break boys and break girls, largely improvisational soloist performers who danced in the breaks of the music (Starr and Waterman 377).

These singular performances were in contrast to other popular dances of the time such as "the freak," where a male and a female would dance closely together as though in a sandwich and often provocatively (Hagar 38). The rhythmic base of the music allowed for the mixing of dance movements that increased in complexity as the breaks were elongated. Breaking became popular at parties, disco clubs, and talent shows as a highly unstructured form of spontaneous dancing. Though these are the historical roots of the term, what the "break" in *b-boy* or *b-girl* signifies is fluid. Some even suggest that the dancer has a temporary break where he or she loses his or her mind in order to move to the music (Schloss, "Foundation" 59).

Other DJs besides Kool Herc would take these techniques further, including Grandmaster Flash (aka Joseph Saddler) who was known for his speed mixes and generally played in the central and south Bronx. Influenced by Kool Herc, Flash was a resident of the Bronx, having moved with his family from the West Indies. He used headphones to synchronize the sounds between records, thereby "pre-cuing" beats in between records to maintain a steady beat by stitching together the sounds of drums from the original songs. The speed and accuracy of his mixes, putting together the beats from one song to another, earned him the name "Flash" as he was known for spinning his records backward rapidly (Price 156). Listening to the beats via

Grandmaster Flash during the Rock and Roll Hall of Fame induction ceremony, 2007. (AP Photo/Seth Wenig.)

headphones allowed the DJ to more precisely pinpoint the breaks in the music, starting and stopping them seamlessly.

In terms of musical development, Grandmaster Flash is also credited as the first DJ to begin pre-cuing and back spinning on records (Hagar 36) as well as to practice moves with MCs to keep the crowd entertained. Flash was known for using the Furious Five, a group of MCs, to keep his parties going (Rahn 3). The Furious Five were added gradually, beginning with Cowboy (aka Keith Wiggins), Kidd Creole (aka Danny Glover), and his brother Melle Mel (Melvin Glover); these were Grandmaster Flash's three MCs. The group soon grew to include Duke Bootree (aka Ed Fletcher) and Kurtis Blow (aka Kurtis Walker).

The group went through several transitions, replacing members with newcomers and trying commercial success with Sugar Hill Records, the producers of what would become known as the first rap single. The group's MC, Melle Mel, was one of the earliest MCs to create a name for himself due to his powerful lyrics and is often credited with being the earliest modern MC. Melle Mel and his other MCs were known for rhyming back and forth between themselves to the beat, creating a mix between the rhyme and the rhythm (Bradley 14). This was one of the earliest examples of MCing to the beat rather than sporadically calling out into the crowd. The effect was a syncopated sound which blended rhythm, image, and storytelling to create meaning from the seemingly spontaneous words of the MC. Prior to his work as an MC, Melle Mel was also a well-known b-boy whom some classified as part of the second wave of b-boying (Fitzgerald 69–77). Contract disputes between Melle Mel and Grandmaster Flash, as well as the death of Cowboy, one of the first three MCs, kept the group from attaining commercial success (Price 156–157). But Flash's outdoor parties, often held at 169th Street and Boston Road, are where many a "battle" or dance off between rival crews was staged. The group's recording "The Message" (1982) included reflections on life in their neighborhood, an urban setting as a political message, establishing one of the trends of early hip hop artists as socially conscious and willing to deal with sensitive subject matter (Cheney 8). Between Melle Mel and Duke Bootie, the challenges of life unfold:

> You'll grow in the ghetto, living second-rate,
> And your eyes will sing a song of deep hate.

As one of the earliest musical recordings in the rap genre, it was also a blend of social protest and cultural reflection of the issues facing those who lived in American's landscape. It was the first song to be defined as a "message" rap (Wheeler 195) or have a socially conscious element in its lyrics. The single would come to define "old school" hip hop, which is now generally believed to have flourished from 1977 to 1987 (Dyson and Daulatzai 4). The trend of hip hop music featuring social protest or serving as an active vehicle to resist racism, discrimination, police brutality, or other social ills would become a separate strand within the rapid development of rap music.

Hip hop music and dance were the ideal tools for an inquisitive teenager to devote his or her energy and in return gain a sense of identity, belonging, and place without danger or violence. Boys in their teens were mentored by older dancers, DJs, MCs, or graffiti artists. The DJ was a constant source of musical innovation as Grand Wizard Theodore (aka Theodore) proved with his introduction of "scratching" or incorporating the sound of the record as it was spun into the rhythm of the beats he created (Hagar 38). The scratch came from sliding a needle across the surface of the record, allowing the DJ to lift a part of a song or sound (Aldridge 229). Anecdotally the story goes that Theodore discovered his technique because of being interrupted by his mother one day while playing a record too loudly at home. Placing his finger on the record in order to respond to her, the scratch was born (Morgan, "Real Hip Hop" 201). Being introduced to DJing at 13, even at that young age Theodore was known to practice his mixing abilities continuously. This technique, pioneered in Grand Wizard Theodore's bedroom, created a percussive sound effect which crowds of dancers came to love. A student of Grandmaster Flash and his brother, Grand Wizard Theodore also developed techniques to drop the needle in various spots on the record (Black Dot xv). Grand Wizard Theodore was among a crew of MCs and DJs who would be one of the earliest rap groups (1980). Many refer to Flash and the Furious Five as among the foundational groups in the development of hip hop music with the DJ at the musical center, aided by his MCs. The DJ was a type of cultural hero in the mid 1970s as he traveled to parties as a freelancer with his sound system and records (Hagar 33) encouraging crowds to dance the night away.

The Roots of the Moves

Each b-boy or b-girl had to make sure his or her moves were ready for competition as battles were central to establishing the reputation of a crew. Break dancing competitively in a crew meant the chance to establish showmanship as well as respect from other crews and the audience. The advent of hip hop music meant that disco-inspired movements such as the hustle, a line dance that included salsa-like foot movements, were replaced by hand movements and dance interludes such as "burning" or "going off," when one dancer would take the floor and demonstrate his or her prowess. Much like the graffiti writer, a b-boy or b-girl wanted to rise above the competition with a "burn." The crossover terminology is an example of how intertwined dance, graffiti, and the music were in the 1970s as a hip hop aesthetic was being created. Early break dance techniques were borrowed from a range of sources. For example, the "flare" was named after a men's gymnastics move on the pommel horse. Other inspiration came from disco moves such as the drops and spins by disco artists such as

James Brown. B-boys had signature moves which they could name themselves after, much like the tags used by graffiti writers.

The various styles within hip hop dance reflect its diverse roots, including the blend of cultural practices such as martial arts and Afro-Caribbean tradition. The other key influences on hip hop dance were the four major variations of dance in America in the late 1960s and early 1970s, including break dancing, the electric boogie, locking, and funk (Engle 363). Across the four categories is a range of choices used by each dancer to create an overall effect. The goal in hip hop dance was to use various parts of the body purposefully while giving the impression of fluidity through a wide range of motion. In addition to hands and feet, as well as stern facial expressions to give off "attitude," the dancer could choose which parts in his or her spine to contract, for example, to create a certain effect of sharp or smooth movements (Engle 363). Break dancing focuses on isolated movements of the body, while in doing the electric boogie a dancer moved his or her entire body in a sequence (Banes 152).

Locking, however, used the illusion that a dancer's joints are stuck in place while other body parts swing wildly, as in the move "the robot," when someone would swing his or her arm, bent at the elbow. Popping, by contrast, is when only one segment of the body moves while the rest stays still. The dancer moves in a quick, abrupt contraction through various body parts, including ribs, shoulders, or neck (LaBoskey 113). The dancer's muscle control is showcased in fast and rhythmic isolation.

Popping and locking were executed in a mime-like way where the dancer created an illusion for the audience. Both popping and locking were made famous on the television show *Soul Train* through the moves of the appropriately named group, the Lockers, originally known as the Campbellock Dancers after their founder, Don Campbell (Banes 151). The variety program came to Los Angles in 1971 (ending in 2006) and became a televised forum where talented dancers could showcase their skills to the nation at large. With a largely African American following, it was one of the few shows of the 1970s to feature black culture in terms of fashion, music, and dance. It featured disco and funk music at a time when the other popular television variety show was *American Bandstand*, geared towards a mainstream and largely white viewership. One of the group's members, Jeffrey Daniel, is credited with practicing and popularizing the moonwalk before Michael Jackson immortalized it. While all these elements could be fused into a routine, it was ultimately up to the dancer to decide on which dance techniques to use and, perhaps more importantly, how to demonstrate flair and talent by infusing the moves with his or her individual interpretation.

Martial arts films were another source of inspiration. The emphasis on rhythm and style, as well as movements using the whole body executed close to the ground, were common to break dancing and fighting techniques used by martial arts masters and actors like Brue Lee (Holman 39). While performing the Brooklyn Uprock, for example, a dancer would stop all movement and drop to the ground in a kung fu–style movement (Green 23–25). Moves such as the "slingshot," where the dancer would drop to the floor and come up, miming that he or she was holding a slingshot, became increasingly popular (Hagar 32). The steps or drops to the ground mimicked the fighting sequences in movies by kung fu legends such as Bruce Lee, which further dramatized the battle element of competitive break dancing. The freeze was designed to extend a particular move and maximize the prowess of the performer, thereby extending the humiliation of his or her opponent (Tanz 48). Each individual could be evaluated across a host of categories including enthusiasm, creativity, coordination, and rhythm. The irony of competitive break dancing became that the crews had likely done hours of preparation in order to look as though they were unrehearsed and spontaneous.

Floor work was the heart of any dance and was often improvised to the music provided by the DJ. In the 1970s, break dancing became popular among African American youth; it was fueled by competition, largely undertaken by Puerto Rican youth in crews (Nelson 15). The goal was always the same: to outperform one's opponent by outlasting them or using more daring or tricky moves. Various subsets of the Bronx community would hold contests in gyms and centers including Saint Martin's church on 182nd Street and Cortona Avenue. These breaking contests came to replace fighting as a means of handling urban conflict (Hagar 87). B-boys came to brand themselves according their clothing and signature moves on the dance floor: King Uprock (aka Ralph Casanova) won his title after an uprock battle for the title of first place in Brooklyn in 1980 (Tanz 46). Breakers and their crews began performing regularly in clubs all over New York City, including the Negril, Danceteria, and the Kitchen (Banes 131).

Joe-Joe (aka Joe Torres), whom many credit with having invented the backspin, founded the Rock Steady Crew in 1977 along with Jimmy D (Price 32). Hailing from the Bronx, the original Rock Steady Crew still has members around the world in local chapters. Notable members include Prince Ken Swift, or K-Swift (aka Kenny Gabbert), who was known for his lighting-fast footwork and freeze style, or "downrock," as anything on the floor was commonly referred to. Named for the uprock move "the rock," the crew and its members would come to occupy a defining space in the world of b-boying as originators of some of the first dance moves, as well as film appearances. They were also the first crew recorded to have a female member, Bunny Lee, the girlfriend of one of the members. K-Swift and his crew were part of what many would define as the third wave of b-boys (Fitzgerald 69–77).

The influence of the group on youngsters in the community was evident when a young b-boy asked to start a Manhattan chapter of the group. Crazy Legs (Richie Colon), at the time barely a teenager, would go from establishing a neighborhood chapter to being president of the Rock Steady Crew. Named for his loose-limbed signature entry into the circle, Crazy Legs is still an active b-boy today. The Rock Steady Crew remains active in breaking, making it one of the few original crews to survive from the 1970s. It was Crazy Legs who went around the city, asking who the best b-boys were and trying to drum up interest in practicing moves. With chapters in Japan, Canada, and the United States, Crazy Legs holds one of the most established reputations for b-boying in break dancing history, beginning with cameos in iconic films of the 1980s. He is credited with inventing the backspin, as well as the continuous backspin or "windmill," as the move became commonly referred to (FNV Newsletter).

The Rock Steady Crew's reputation as performers and their savvy managers led to their being invited to display their talents before the Queen of England at a fundraiser and the first break dancers to perform at Carnegie Hall (Price 181). Yet these early commercial appearances by the Rock Steady Crew would hint at coming conflicts in the marketing and promotion of hip hop; the group recorded a song, "Hey You Rock Steady Crew," that they were given margin rights for; their managers organized public appearances that often focused on showcasing their talent as opposed to the roots or message of hip hop as a youth-centered, creative culture. These experiences led to

Crazy Legs of the Rock Steady Crew. (AP Photo/Jason DeCrow.)

bitterness toward the media and other parts of the entertainment industry (FNV Newsletter). Eventually invited by Afrika Bambaataa to become members of his Zulu Nation, the Rock Steady Crew appeared in all the major films and significant publications about break dancing in the 1980s.

Ethnic Influences

In the first phase of the development of hip hop culture, in the Bronx in the 1970s, the influence of West Indian and Latino—particularly Puerto Rican—youth was as significant as the participation of African Americans. Later this would change as the perception of hip hop came to be dominated by the sense that it was the outpouring of African American males. Graffiti and breaking had participants from the diverse ethnic mix of the Bronx neighborhoods; DJing and MCing, however, eventually took on a distinctively African American flair following interest by the recording industry (Rivera 60).

A B-boy's Routine

There are four categories of moves that provide the foundation to breaking; those which are preformed while standing are considered the moves most visible in the 1970s and were later added to by crews like the Rock Steady Crew in the early 1980s to increase the athleticism and showmanship of the dancer. Toprock referred to a set of moves which normally occurred at the start of a routine and was the core of the dance along with ground rock, keeping the dancer upright, standing, in rhythm to the music as filler. The focus is on the footwork, particularly the speed and agility dancer. Toprock was often used as the entrance into the circle by the b-boy or b-girl. While many consider an emphasis on toprock as old school, there are modern b-boys who find it still extremely important to the dance. Smily (aka Danny Dibble) explains how toprock contributes to a b-boy's overall style:

> However top rock and footwork require originality creativity, stamina and a quick mind. I always say that breaking is equal parts mental and physical. In footwork, breakers are expected to take the steps that exist, and combine them into original patterns, creating their own movements. Using concepts such as rotation, momentum, and level changes, footwork and be finessed to be as impressive as any power move. While Ken Swift may not do air flares, he is still amazing anytime he hits the floor. There are infinite combinations of footwork, and those who dedicate themselves to mastering footwork are known as footwork heads or style heads. I myself am a style head ... it's important to make it clear the difficulty involved in becoming fully proficient in footwork, which is an element of breaking largely overlooked by those who don't break. (Dibble)

While not as flashy as power moves or freezes, which come later in a routine, good toprock establishes a dancer's style, as Smily argues: "Footwork and toprock both require being able to think in three dimensions, the ability to create your own moves, and the originality to imbue every individual movement with style, flavor and originality" (Dibble). Following a dancer's entrance into the circle, he or she often begins with improvisation moves in response to the beat of the song, using mocking gestures towards his or her opponent(s), while preparing to go to the floor for power moves. The transition between

toprock and movements executed on the ground if done well could
mean that the one's opponent had to work harder to prove his or her
challenge. Ground rock provides smooth transitions between toprock
and the power moves, which were generally the hardest but were
guaranteed to get reactions from the crowd. The foundation for any
dancer was the footwork—the first thing the audience or the opponent
saw was a b-boy's toprock or those moves done while standing.

The "new school" in breaking involved more acrobatic moves, performed lower to the ground and in sequences of six steps. But power
moves such as glides, windmills, and spins or other acrobatic movements were incorporated to wow the audience and humble one's opponent and could be done consecutively as power combos. They are
considered part of the original breaking moves but were introduced into
the mainstream most notably by the Rock Steady Crew. Soon anything
that could be done in sequence, one after the other, including head
spins, black flips, or movements that involved the dancer spinning or
rotating repeatedly, such as flares where hands and legs move around
the body as the b-boy propels his body weight in a circle on the floor,
were examples of signature battle-winning moves.

Smily explains the variations between the old school and new school
views on breaking further:

> Traditionally, there are two schools of thought within breaking which
> have only recently begun to be reconciled. The conservative school of
> breaking, made up largely of the older generation breakers, holds that
> breaking should reflect one's own style and flavor, and heavily
> emphasize the foundational movements that were laid down in New
> York in the 70s and 80s. The opposing school, made up of mostly new
> school breakers, believe that breakers should push the boundaries of
> what the human body is able to do. This has led to a large amount of
> b-boys to specialize, becoming proficient in one area and giving
> up the other. I myself chose to become a style head, and dedicate myself
> to mastering all elements of footwork, flavor, and originality in
> breaking.
>
> In recent years, there has been a reconciliation of sorts. Around 2005,
> b-boys were made more aware of the importance of footwork and top-
> rock, as well as character and flavor. This led to a trend in breaking where
> many students, (myself included), chose to focus on style. In competi-
> tions, those who lacked basic toprock and footwork skills, and only pos-
> sessed amazing power moves, are no longer able to win. In recent

years, since 2008, b-boys have trended to become more well rounded, and are expected to possess not only footwork but power moves as well. This trend was largely brought about by competitions. (Dibble)

Though Smily and other b-boys are in support of a good uprock, there seems to be an accepted bias towards power moves, particularly among those new to breaking: "If a purely power dancer goes up against a purely style dancer, the winner will be determined by the judge's bias. Since 2005, judges usually gave it to the style b-boy. People unfamiliar to breaking are likely to give the battle to the dancer using power" (Dibble).

This may be because according to many b-boys, including Slinky (aka Bryan Boyer) power moves are the hardest of all to perform and perfect. As a dancer on cruise liners, he explains, " . . . the hardest to learn and take the most practice are Power moves. . . . The reason being is that you're throwing your body in the air hoping to land correctly on your hands or risk possible injury. . . . I take a lot of risks and have to practice them daily to make certain I have it perfected" (Boyer). Perhaps the most challenging of these is the thread or windmill flare, referring to when the legs alternate swinging in a V through the hands by sheer force of the b-boy's building momentum. Other variations of flares include swinging legs together instead of apart, swinging only one leg instead of both, supporting the body with one arm instead of two or leaning on the elbow of one arm or the shoulders instead of the hands. The finish of a flare can bring the dancer to his or her hands or onto his or her back; the more complex the move, the more experience and practice the b-boy needs in order to avoid injury.

Freezes stopped all motion and were extended poses that occurred towards the end of the routine. Popular freezes to conclude with included headstands, single handstands, or sitting postures, including the most challenging ones that involved one half of the body—head, shoulder and arm—holding up the other, as in the shoulder freeze. The most common form of breaking involved the four types of steps in sequence: entering the circle, uprock footwork, followed by a freeze, and exit. At first these individual turns in the circle lasted 10 to 30 seconds. The freeze was the most important moment during a b-boy's appearance in the circle and, while practiced extensively before competing, it could be chosen at random depending on the moves of the other dancer (Banes 146). High school b-boy ChuckyyJei (aka Jasper

Sanchez) believes that freezes may be the hardest of all the moves because "It takes a much greater amount of skill, concentration, and strength to be able to hold many types of freezes" (Sanchez). He believes a good breaker will have proficiency in all of the various moves: toprock, footwork, power moves, and freezes. His introduction into b-boying was similar to that of the early teenage b-boys on the streets of New York: he was amazed by the efforts of those he saw break dancing and "[was] astonished by how cool they looked" (Sanchez).

B-boys and b-girls are assessed on their attitude, originality, and stamina during a routine that often requires sudden bursts of energy, a certain level of athleticism, flexibility, and endurance (Green 43–67). In order to be able to perform the various moves as well as excel during battles, b-boys are expected to be in good health: dancing for hours on end is a type of workout in and of itself, but to achieve some of the more advanced moves, pushups, weight lifting, and other athletic training distinguished the best from those who were just starting out.

The foundations of a good breaking routine remain the same around the world as b-boy Tasty (aka Kamil Saňák) from Prague, Czech Republic, explains:

> B-boying is about expressing yourself and without foundations you can't create your style. . . . If you have no flow, then you are not b-boy! And only b-boy who has good toprock and footwork can have good flow and also flava. Flava is your character in your dance . . . so most important are foundations of toprock and footwork . . . as hardest you practice them as good b-boy you can be. . . . It's also good to put some freezes and power in your flow . . . that makes your sets variable and more interesting . . . but if you have no flow, even though you have all powers, than you are not b-boy . . . just some gymnast. (Saňák)

Ayhan Adem Gültekin agrees with Tasty that proficiency in all four types of steps is central to a good b-boy: "Honestly a b-boy who want to be number one, must do every style (I mean toprock, freeze, footwork, power moves, chair, trix)" (Gültekin). Ayhan, who is a member of the Turkish crew the Istanbul Style Breakers, learned his moves while studying in Korea. There seems to be a sort of consensus on this importance of the toprock to the b-boy, as Allen Maverick G. Mapue attempts to define what a b-boy is and isn't: "I think many dancers

nowadays call themselves 'B-boys' but they only knew how to do flips.
... I think it's not right. You may know how to flip but it's not actually
a proof that you are already a b-boy" (Mapue).

Battling among Crews

Dance became an alternative means by which youth in urban New
York settled their differences rather than through physical contact.
Instead of gangs, crews became a type of alternate family for their
members, further identified by their unique dress and new names
(Leland 254). A crew or posse would generally be from the same
neighborhood or block and were units of local social identity for youth
(Starr and Waterman 377). Groups would form into crews by neighborhood and "battle" against one another for dominance on the dance
floor and for a reputation as the best performers. Crews were teams
competing in the same spirit as sports teams for prestige and recognition (LaBoskey 114). A typical battle involved two b-boys or their
entire crews in alternating demonstrations of their prowess. In general
the dancers saved their best moves for the end of the dance, in order to
take the other crew by surprise. Emphasis during these competitions
was on the entrance of the dancers, their toprock or standing moves,
and the transition from toprock to their ground moves, which showcased the power. The finish or end of the performance was another
opportunity to hide an element of surprise to raise the bar that the
other crew would struggle to match. Facial expressions were also
incorporated in these routines to further heighten the character of
the overall performance. The crews would take turns until one side
ran out of moves, and the winners were usually those who were
cleaner in their overall performance and used the most difficult moves
overall (Green 105–106). "Razzing moves" or insulting gestures were
a part of competitions when the challenger could directly address his
or her opponent. A dancer would generally open with razzing as these
are classified as uprock movements, or those performed while standing upright at the start of the dance, used to insult the opponent
(Banes 17). The goal is to show one's sense of rhythm and style before
going to the floor in power moves to demonstrate power and speed.
The symbolism in uprock is that of two dancers, in the 1970s usually
male, facing off against each other as in the heat of a gang show down.

They move towards each other in aggressive ways but the tension only mounts because they never actually engage in violence (Tokaji 103). Through breaking, the ability to establish superiority without violence was available—though depending on the size of the crew and the battle, it was not always guaranteed that things would remain peaceful.

Gaining entry into a crew was not easy or taken for granted; often dancers had to battle in order to become accepted by the crew, showing how their personality was exhibited on the dance floor and could further strengthen the crew's reputation. Nicknames were commonly given for the signature move of a particular b-boy or b-girl in the style of comic book characters. Someone who was good at holding a particular position for a long time, known as a freeze, for example, could be called Dr. Freeze (Green 107). By holding a freeze, the b-boy extended his performance, and the longer he could hold it, the more challenging the move to his competitor. The freeze and other moves became the signature of the break dancing movement. Crews often utilized an apprenticeship system whereby a new b-boy could learn maneuvers and techniques and receive other mentoring from more seasoned dancers. During the heyday of interest in break dancing, tours and brand endorsements were not uncommon.

The ability of a crew to synchronize and employ a variety of spatial patterns—different levels and formations during a performance—increased their chances of winning a battle. Battles were a way to be seen, heard, and remembered as the winners of a competition in the neighborhood—important to the identity and self-esteem of most of the teenage members of the crews, who were otherwise living in the margins of society.

The Ghettoriginals were a crew whose tour was sponsored by the brand Calvin Klein (Nelson 14) and had a female member, Rockafella (aka Ana Garcia). Rockafella is still b-girling today, having established Full Circle Productions, which continues to promote all aspects of the breaking culture. She talks about the reaction to female dancers inside the circle:

> I also noticed this was not how they handled one another—man to man. Among the guys it was either straight respect or straight battle of skills. . . . a guy grabbed me and thought he would hump me, I straddled my legs around his waist and then did a back walk over.

I eased out of his grip and slid between his legs. Then I proceeded to mock him by slapping his ass and kicking him out the circle.... I realized if I could conquer the floor, the guys would have to wait until I was finished or risk getting hurt. They'd have to think twice before tryin' it. And so began my quest for floor moves.... (Garcia 58)

Women did participate in crews, and many members of the Rock Steady Crew were b-girls, including Baby Love (aka Daisy Castro); their inclusion was not as widespread as the established presence of the b-boy on the dance floor. One of the few all-female crews in the 1980s was the Dynamic Dolls, who came out of the larger, mostly male crew the Dynamic Breakers. Kim-a-Kazi (aka Kim Valente) was one of the members of this rare all-female crew who toured with Run-DMC as well as appearing in breaking movies such as *Beat Street* (though she left after a few days of taping for professional reasons). Using continuous choreography while performing rather than watching the member in the middle of the circle, the group performed the popular moves of the day including power moves and freezes used by b-boys. The Dynamic Dolls were also part of the well-known performance at the Kennedy Center to which all the breakers received a standing ovation.

B-Girls in the Twenty-First Century

Perhaps one of the most ironic developments in breaking is the resurgence of breaking internationally but among women. From the late 1990s, b-girls have been forming crews, hosting their own battles, and in general enjoying a revival of old school breaking long after breaking was a key element of pop culture. Florida based b-boy Michael Burton explains how b-girls are made welcome in the contemporary breaking circle: "The amount of b-girls is growing pretty fast ... showing that women are just as capable as men at breaking. As a matter of fact, crews usually use girls as their killers or finishers in battles because of their uniqueness" (Burton). The support for b-girls from modern b-boys seems to be fairly widespread. Smily (aka Danny Dibble), a b-boy in the California Bay Area, agrees:

In breaking, girl breakers generally receive more props than male breakers. In my view, girl breakers are judged solely relative to other girl breakers. Lately, there have been many b-girl only battles, which may appear at the same event as a b-boy battle. This in my mind is a good idea. In sports there are boy leagues and girl leagues, and breaking is such a physically dependent activity that it should follow that breaking should be organized much the same. However, in group battles, b-girls sometimes battle against b-boys. This in my eyes is unfair to the b-boys, because the b-girls will receive more props because of their gender. (Dibble)

The feeling that the b-girl and her moves are special is not just an American sentiment, as b-boy Allen Maverick G. Mapue from the Philippines explains: "I idolize more a b-girl because it takes a lot of confidence and determination for the woman to learn. We all know that majority of girls are scared of stunts like freezes, power moves" like" (Mapue). ChuckyyJei (aka Jasper Sanchez) would go as far as to say that anyone who practices and is dedicated to learning b-boying or b-girling will improve: "Breakdancing does not discriminate against gender at all whatsoever" (Sanchez).

Established as We B* Girlz, an international network of b-girls who gather annually for festivals in Berlin with competitions and workshops, the modern b-girl community is made up of vibrant female entrepreneurs who not only dance themselves but have founded dance companies and studios to train and inspire others. Supported by Martha Cooper, the photographer who immortalized subway graffiti and remains active in b-girl culture, *We B* Girlz* is also the title of a book about female breakers, showcasing their performances and practices from 2004 onward. Other notable b-girl movements in the United States include the B-Girl Be: A Celebration of Women in Hip-Hop annual conference sponsored by the Intermedia Arts organization in Minneapolis, Minnesota. Since 2005, the B-Girl Be summit has gathered together hundreds of women interested in the foundational elements of hip hop and offered workshops, seminars, and networking opportunities for those interested in perfecting their breaking skills (Hobson and Bartlow 5).

Asia One, of No Easy Props Productions, is one such example of a b-girl who has not only embraced breaking for herself but also helped organized workshops and conferences for others including the well-established, decade-plus B-Boy Summit, which is an annual international gathering for all members of the breaking community.

We B*Girlz break dancers at Lincoln Center, 2006. (AP Photo/Frank Franklin II.)

She got her start in the early 1990s by performing in Colorado at a Denver hip hop show. She pursued her training with the LA chapter of the Rock Steady Crew; she is one of the central female figures in the modern breaking scene, active in promoting breaking around the world through performances, training, and writing about b-girl culture.

Momz-N-Da-Hood is perhaps one of the most unique examples of b-girls to date—a group of mothers in their 40s and 50s who are still breaking. Many of them got their exposure to breaking as young women in New York in the 1970s and describe breaking as being a casually observed street art by passersby—people never imagined being watched or watching others on television or in the movies. Barbara Alder, dance captain of Momz-N-Da-Hood, says that she is proud of all the b-girls they see on the scene now when their group goes to competitions. She sees the contemporary break dancing community as gender neutral. For the group, the most challenging moves are the power moves because of the agility and flexibility they require. Alder comments: "The moves that we find the most challenging are the power moves (Windmill, Turtle Freezes, etc.) but they are the most fun for us to learn, because no one in a million years would expect to see a 50 year old Mom spinning on her back!" (Alder). She believes that dance allows a common language, whether between the Momz and their children or as dancers and their audiences. Alder also warns against the toll that power moves can have on one's body in the long run as the impact of spinning on extremities can damage the body:

> "old timers" . . . talk about injuries and body degradation they have suffered over the years. Knee replacements, hip problems, neuropathy in their hands, neck issues. . . . [I am] seeing the bar being raised higher and higher from the young breakdancing community. I am seeing kids tossing themselves onto their heads, deathdrops, and several other jaw dropping moves that DO have serious risks to their physical well being. (Alder)

But with active dancers in the United States, United Kingdom, and other parts of the world, b-girls of all ages congregate annually in Berlin to show off their skills and compete for the title of champion. Many b-girls interested in seeing the traditions of breaking continue have gone on to establish their own dance companies. B-girl Firefly (aka Andrea Parker) is one such example of dancer turned entrepreneur. Founder of the UK-based Firefly Associates, Parker has competed professionally against men as well as women. The company specializes in break dancing workshops and entertainment as well as training teachers on how to use break dancing techniques in schools with their students.

Then there are women like Lady Jules (aka Julie Ulrich) who have uploaded videos onto open-access Web sites such as eHow.com that show beginners how to learn to break dance. Ulrich's 10 videos on the site demonstrate in step-by-step process, along with detailed explanations, how to execute everything from backspins to the basic six-step footwork moves. Ulrich is a well-known b-girl and also a trained professional dancer, performing with the hip hop influence Rennie Harris Puremovement Dance Company. Dance companies such as Firefly Associates and Puremovement bring hip hop movements, training workshops, and dance techniques to aspiring breakers and audiences in Europe and around the world.

Ulrich also starred in the short film *B-GIRL* which features the story of Angel, a passionate young dancer who is forced to move from the East Coast to LA after being attacked. Dancing may have been the cause of her exposure to danger, but in her new life Angel can't seem to separate herself or create a new identity outside of dance. The movie channels her journey to finding the dance scene in LA and reconnecting with the most vital part of her—her dancing. The filmmaker and producer explain that their reasoning behind making the film was a desire to portray the experiences of b-girls in a realistic and ethical way by using only real breakers and thereby preserving an element of authenticity of the b-boy community. The film has been shown all over the country at over 20 festivals and also in Europe.

Carla Stalling Huntington sees b-boying, b-girling, and hip hop dance in general as an egalitarian form of artistic expression where the roles for male or female dancers are not prescribed. She draws a distinction between commercialized hip hop dance (rap videos or movies) and uncommercialized hip hop dance. She argues that hip hop dancing in nightclubs or in live performance is empowering for both the male and female dancer:

> Uncommercialized hip hop dance...has never set forth practices portraying men hating women. The dances are not like ballet where men and women have particular roles to play on a stage and men are dominant while women are weak. They are social dances that set up partners as equal...dance that is staged often shows African American men and women performing the same movement vocabulary....in dance clubs...if you want to dance, you dance. (93)

Whether a b-girl or a b-boy, the contemporary breaker learns about break dancing via technological innovations featuring breaking, including the Internet via YouTube and commercial media such as DVDs or television shows. B-boy Y-ray (aka Wairhe Napoleon) of Nigeria, for example, first saw someone breaking via DVD:

> I got into the dance known as b-boying after watching a b-boy Dvd which I borrowed from a friend, when I saw what these boys and girls were doing, my mind was blown, the music flowed into my heart, I was inspired at that moment and so it lead me into the dance which I do today, ever since then I started improving my moves. B-boying isn't just an art or a hobby but it's also a way of expression in which mediums like radio and TV cannot express it adequately. We dance to express not impress. (Napoleon)

Shana Busmente of the Philippines credits the movie *Step Up 2* with inspiring her to be a b-girl. Whether in the Philippines or Nigeria, breaking is still gaining new dancers around the world. Not unsurprisingly, they are teenagers who are familiar with its American roots but feel they also have something to contribute to the art form. Most modern breakers, male and female, are mostly optimistic about what the future holds for breaking. As 19-year-old b-boy Michael Burton says, "Breaking is not the same anymore. There are so many new ideas that this generation is hatching that previous generations would have deemed impossible. The hip hop culture is on the verge a major shift for the better" (Burton). Johnny Lee, one of the executive producers of *Planet B-boy*, agrees that this is a good time for female breakers as well as awareness that breaking is a viable art form:

> As far as I have seen, there are definitely less female breakers than male. While that is clear, the female breakers receive such a large amount of respect and admiration from the whole b-boying community that it is difficult for me to say that b-girls have a more difficult time. Recently, a movie titled "B-Girl" was produced and screened here in America. Projects like that and Planet B-boy will hopefully help more b-girls find more acceptance from their families who do not yet realize it is more than just a street dance that street kids do. (Lee)

Films, documentaries, and the popularity of shows such as *So You Think You Can Dance* have brought break dancing and hip hop dance back into the modern dance scene and ensured their popularity among young urban dancers as well as continued to give them a broader public platform than the streets of the various neighborhoods where they began. Breaking inspired a teenager in Penticton, British Columbia, Canada via television. Popping Stan (aka Stanley Satoria) credits television for his induction to b-boying: "I saw [on *So You Think You Can Dance*] an amazing popper named "Phillip 'Pacman' Chbeeb"! He was so dope that I wanted to dance like him. . . . my sister introduced me to take dance classes! I always wanted to learn how to pop, but at the same time, I thought it would be cool to learn how to lock and break! And that is how I started breaking!" (Satoria).

The benefits of breaking have not changed from the early days of youth culture in the Bronx among Puerto Ricans and African Americans; it still appeals largely to teenagers—albeit now with an international audience—because of a search for identity, community, and relief from boredom or to be cool. As ChuckyyJei of Santa Clara, California, explains:

> I think it's [break dancing] a terrific way to meet new people, become more athletic and work out. It will keep you in fit condition as long as

A performer from the *So You Think You Can Dance*/Party City 4th Annual Halloween Bash in San Francisco. (Tony Avelar/AP Images for Party City.)

you practice often. Many people think it is too difficult for them to attempt at first hand, but once you get started I find it hard to stop. I believe it helps one gain muscle, concentration, and self confidence. (Sanchez)

Even in as unlikely a place as Jeddah, Saudi Arabia, breaking crews are thriving. Says Jooda, a b-boy in Saudi Arabia, "for today's dancers, they have better places than the old school dancers places [to perform]" (Jooda).

Firmly planted in the mainstream by 1997, break dancing was being performed at concerts and malls, far from its origins on the streets of New York. It appeared break dancing and hip hop were no longer a subculture but part of mainstream America.

2

From Urban to Suburban

While the 1980s unfolded, a series of events combined to give break dancing more attention in the mainstream media including a front-page article in *The Village Voice* on b-boying, coverage on the television news show *20/20*, recognition of the music by critics, and growing interest in the "battles" between crews for the reputation as the best breaker. Perhaps the most notorious of these battles was between the Rock Steady Crew and the Dynamic Rockers in 1982 at the Lincoln Center, with the Rock Steady Crew emerging as the winner. The battle was barely seen by audiences because the crews each brought so many members of their posses to back them up; they crowded the dance circle, obscuring the b-boys and the competition from the view of the onlookers. Equally important was the coverage of the event by noted New York publications as well as *National Geographic*. The presence of break dancing crews and hip hop style were introduced to the nation at large.

While b-boying began in the South Bronx, a similar interest in hip hop dance was flowering in California, on the West Coast. These differences in origin and style were the precursors to others differences in East Coast versus West Coast style that would soon be replicated in the burgeoning rap industry in the 1990s. Yet, unlike the genre distinctions in music, breaking, popping, and locking would all be lumped together by the media under the broad category of break

A break dancing battle at Vision Art Hall in Los Angeles, part of the Ghetto Muisk Three talent showcase. (AP Photo/ Chad K. Uyeno.)

dancing. The roots of West Coast hip hop were tied to funk music but did rely on groups or crews when performing. The main basis of West Coast hip hop were the popping and locking movements made popular by the Campbell Lockers. Another popular group, similar to the Rock Steady Crew in that members are still active today, is the Electric Boogaloos. Both East Coast and West Coast dance styles are a series of highly improvised movements which are designed to show off the creativity of the performer.

In 1981, as mainstream media including the *Village Voice* and the *New York Times* began to take note of these battles, break dancing gained prominence as a working-class tool of expression and advancement (Tanz 53). The media attention on what was once urban street dancing caused a flurry of interest around the nation. This interest was not without its challenges, however. In newspapers and films the representations of the art form began to shift away from the organic "b-boy" culture that originated hip hop into content with an appeal for a mass market. By the end of the decade, commercialization of two key elements of hip hop, b-boying and rapping, would change the landscape of American music and dance forever.

Breaking on Television and in Film

One of the crescendo moments nearly didn't happen: the inclusion of a short set featuring break dancing in what would become the 1980s' most popular film on dancing and youth expression—*Flashdance*. Originally the b-boys needed convincing that a movie appearance was a good idea. The connection between what they did on the streets of New York on their own time and the interest in the movie industry did not match up. In the end they were persuaded by their manager, Kool Lady Blue (aka Ruza Blue) and the appearance fee, about a thousand dollars each in exchange for performing a brief segment of their moves. The inclusion of four of the most well-known and experienced members of the Rock Steady Crew—Crazy Legs (aka Richie Colon), Ken Swift (aka Kenneth Gabbert), Frosty Freeze (aka Wayne Frost), and Mr. Freeze (aka Marc Lemberger)—ensured that people outside of New York began to take notice of the burgeoning art form (Tanz 53). Their hard-won fame came from street battles, mostly against mostly Puerto Ricans; the 76-second cameo in the movie *Flashdance* in 1983 catapulted break dancing from an urban, street performance into the national imagination. The cameo performance led to the advent of break dancing into more homes across America as the moves were picked up and used by others on MTV videos. Another early promoter of break dancing and hip hop culture, Michael Holman, brought both the music and the dancers into the downtown clubs of Manhattan from the surrounding boroughs (Fricke and Ahearn xiv).

In the early 1980s Holman produced a hip hop television show, *Graffiti Rock*, which only aired one episode. The plan for the show was to feature the up-and-coming artists of hip hop, including DJs, MCs, and breakers, namely the New York City Breakers, the crew that Holman managed. He hired a graffiti artist to decorate the set's backdrop; Afrika Bambaataa recommended the DJ, and Run-DMC was the first group to perform on the pilot. While Holman could see the potential in the emerging hip hop market, and the show premiered to positive reviews, national syndication proved elusive. Television executives had a difficult time understanding the distinction between *Graffiti Rock* and the long-running *Soul Train*, so the series folded. It is still remembered as one of the pioneers of hip hop culture, bringing the foundational elements together into homes across the country, if only briefly.

The advent of MTV, Music Television, as a cable channel which featured music videos and a VJ, or videojockey, to introduce various videos soon became a fixture of youth culture in the 1980s. To have break dancing and hip hop music featured on this emerging medium only gave these urban genres glamour as well as legitimacy. Videos became the primary mode of promotion for the recording industry as well as for the circulation and consumption of imagery, ideas, and artists in popular culture from the 1980s onwards (Emerson 133).

Other films on break dancing were soon to follow in the mid-1980s, including the PBS documentary *Style Wars* (1983), *Beat Street* (1984), and *Breakin'* (1984), followed by *Breakin' 2: Electric Boogaloo* (1984). Each of these films, from *Flashdance* to *Breakin' 2*, featured young, earnest protagonists from working-class backgrounds who were trying to get recognition for their talent from formal institutions. The medium of cinema worked to change the performance of the dance since room had to be made to include the camera and equipment. The dancers were requested to adapt the tight competitors' circle in order to allow the battling scenes to be filmed. These were the first few steps from breaking as a participatory act into performance art for spectators (Banes 130).

The documentary *Style Wars* highlighted a famous battle between the Rock Steady Crew and the Dynamic Rockers from Queens. The scene featured both crews and their acrobatics-inspired dance moves, and it was filmed in a rollerskating disco (Price 149). Shown at many film festivals, and winning in the documentary category at Sundance, *Style Wars* was an exploration into the multiracial makeup of New York City and the early days of hip hop culture. Like many of the other films that would follow, the directors were able to capture on film people who would later become key figures in hip hop culture: in this instance, Crazy Legs of the Rock Steady Crew. Co-producer Harry Chalfant, one of the first photographers to show an interest in graffiti, along with director Tony Silver, brought the urban canvas and artwork of graffiti writers in the New York subway onto the big screen. Unconventionally, it recorded the work of CAP, a graffiti writer who had no compunctions about tagging over the top of the work of others, much to their dismay and disapproval. The film brought into conversation the teenagers and officials of the city, as well as everyday onlookers such as cops, work crews, and passersby. Silver aptly states the crossover between breaking, writing, and rapping: "The idea of style and competing for the best style is the key to all forms of rocking.

For the rap MC, it's rocking the mike, for the B-boys, it's rocking your body in breakdancing, or, for the writers, rocking the city with your name on a train" (quoted in Sherman 291).

The first film on hip hop culture and break dancing, *Wild Style* (1982), demonstrated the growing interest in the phenomena. It is commonly referred to as the first hip hop movie, in some sense the Hollywood version of *Style Wars*, directed by Charlie Ahearn. It set the trend for using real-life DJs, MCs, graffiti writers, and b-boys as actors in films set in the South Bronx. Notable appearances by the Rock Steady Crew, MCs the Cold Crush Brothers and Grandmaster Caz, and DJs including Grandmaster Flash and Grand Wizard Theodore gave the film a gritty realism. Also included were well-known graffiti writers such as DONDI, whose work decorated the subway cars and opening credits used in the film.

Beat Street showed the intertwined nature of the elements in hip hop culture by featuring four main characters who were graffiti artists and DJs as well as b-boys. Reflecting the multicultural nature of hip hop, three characters were African American—those with DJ and b-boy aspirations—and one, the graffiti writer was Latino. The movies proved that what had begun as an organic and spontaneous means of establishing one's reputation in the urban streets was now material for entertainment (LaBoskey 119). Another significant aspect of the film was the number of DJs and MCs popular at the time and now known as legends in the establishment of hip hop music. The movie included DJ Kool Herc, Grandmaster Melle Mel, and the Furious Five, as well as members from both the Rock Steady Crew and the New York City Breakers.

Major elements of dramatic tension in the film included battles between these crews, showing how film could mimic real life. The storyline itself was somewhat bleak, with one of the protagonists dying in a fight with another graffiti artist in the subway because he finally catches up with his rival, who throughout the entire film keeps writing his tag over newly finished work. The closing frames of the movie, however, show the other characters celebrating the life of their friend in dance as well as song. Breaking, graffiti art, and MCing were all brought into the mainstream media via *Beat Street*, and the film's soundtrack featured hip hop tracks.

Breakin' featured a young Ice-T (aka Tracy Marrow) both as onscreen MC as well as recording artist on the soundtrack. The storyline involves

Scene from the 1980s film *Beat Street*. (Orion Pictures/Photofest.)

a dancer intrigued by breaking and popping to the disapproval of her more traditionally minded teacher. This was a slight reversal on *Flashdance*, where the protagonist is trying to get into the formal academy; here the dancer is trying to build her street credibility (Sherman 292). The focus on street dance meant several scenes showcasing the dexterity and talent of b-boys. The sequel, *Breakin' 2: Electric Boogaloo*, was released in the same year, presumably to capitalize on the interest in break dancing that was sweeping the nation. Not as popular as the first film, the sequel featured a return of the main characters—including Ice-T in his MC role—in a struggle against the city to preserve a neighborhood center.

These movies were set in the urban context of hip hop's roots in the inner city but with a focus on dance as a tool of upward mobility for the working class (Tanz 56). Critics now find flaws in the films as examples of the early commercialization of break dancing diluting the intensity of the socioeconomic roots of the origins of break dancing and hip hop culture—part athletic creativity and part struggle for meaning in the midst of poverty and social alienation. *Beat Street* included a battle performance between the famous Rock Steady

Crew and their notorious rivals, the New York City Breakers, as well as the legendary DJs Afrika Bambaataa and DJ Kool Herc. The inclusion of these established names in hip hop gave the film more credibility than *Breakin'*, for example, which had almost no actual break dancing in the film itself but mostly popping and locking moves. Despite its shortcomings, *Breakin'* would gross $35 million dollars and featured a young Ice-T performing towards the film's end. The depiction of break dancing as a team sport and the highlights of moves by individuals within each crew cemented the inclusion of the former street dance onto dance floors around the country (Nelson 15). The commercial success of the films also established a precedent for white audience members to pay to watch and consume the experiences of street performers and minorities in the inner city, which would later be mimicked in the sales of rap music (Tanz 58).

Break dancing was also featured in commercials for companies including Burger King, Pepsi, Coke, and Panasonic (Banes 14). As the subject of talk shows watched in suburban homes, as well as part of a performance by the New York City Breakers—many of them of Latino origin—at the Kennedy Center attended by President Ronald Reagan as part of his second inaugural festivities, hip hop had arrived very far from its urban roots (Hagar 102). The interest of the mainstream media helped take break dancing from a recreational activity in New York to a commercially viable dance form (Patricia Collins 10).

Flashdance featured a backspin that then became emblematic of break dancing and b-boys. It is no accident that same year, 1983, a pop singer named Michael Jackson learned the moonwalk from a member of the LA crew and immortalized it for millions around the world (Price 114). In 1984, *Newsweek* confirmed the popular interest that break dancing had achieved with a cover story that featured b-boys and b-girls in unlikely states such as Texas and Michigan (Tanz 59). What had begun as improvisational footwork at dance parties was now a national phenomenon associated with teenagers in general. Perhaps at the height of the break dancing fad, the 1984 closing ceremonies of the summer Olympics in LA featured a routine by 200 break dancers, including members of the New York City Breakers (Tanz 65). There was a sense of pride on the part of those who participated in these various events as the rest of the nation could experience positive elements from the Bronx—the same area of New York City reputed to be full of unsavory social elements. Indeed at the time no

one could have predicted that hip hop, which began merely as the
spontaneous creative outlet for the frustration of youth living in urban
blight, would become the source of a worldwide multibillion-dollar
industry. Jam One describes how closely related the four elements of
hip hop were when he was growing up:

> My uncle was a breaker for a while in the late '80s. He gave up but he still
> helped me out with a lot of old-school b-boys. So he'd bring me around to
> the practices and I started meeting some people like that. Then he took
> me to a concert with the Beastie Boys, and I saw Mixmaster Mike there
> and that was the first time I saw somebody scratching, and it blew me
> away I was like I want to do that. (Harkness)

At the same time a sense of excitement was building around the
public discussion of a previously underground culture, a growing rift
was emerging between the energy and creativity which started
b-boying and the perception that break dancing was just another fad
that would quickly come and go. The members of the Rock Steady
Crew featured so prominently in the media weren't sure what to make
of the attention or the fact that their personal styles were now being
mimicked all over the country. Break dancing, a term circulated by
the media, was never really accepted by the hip hop community. The
mania around break dancing materialized as merchandise soon
became available for the average consumer: from how-to demos to
exercise videos, including foldout cardboard squares with slogans for
the aspiring break dancer, head wax, and pads for the hands and
knees, break dancing became a buzzword around the nation. Yet for
those still in the Bronx, this popularization was seen as a limited interpretation of b-boying that diluted the gritty context from which the art
form had emerged. Doctors began warning against the dangers of
break dancing as neck injuries and other medical side effects were felt
by inexperienced individuals. While break dancing reached its heyday
in the mid 1980s, the introduction of hip hop music, however, was just
beginning to take off and would follow a unique trajectory, previously
unseen in the American musical landscape.

The edgy elements of breaking and hip hop dance were seen regularly on television on what was hip hop's first variety show, *In Living
Color*, which aired in the 1990s. A group of versatile and attractive
female dancers, the "Fly Girls," included a young dancer named

Jennifer Lopez who would go on to establish her own recording and acting career. The show was a launching pad for hip hop artists and an answer to the mainstream *Saturday Night Live*. The Fly Girls performed pieces choreographed by Rosie Perez before the commercial breaks in the show and in between skits; their multiethnic membership reflected the broad base of interest in hip hop culture. Of Puerto Rican descent, Perez was a former dancer on *Soul Train* and would go on to choreograph videos by various hip hop artists.

Contemporary television and film has fed the public's continued interest in breaking as a dance form. *America's Best Dance Crew* was produced by Randy Jackson, a judge on the popular series *American Idol*. The show is in its fifth season; it features the opportunity for crews from across the United States to compete for a chance to be among a group of dance crews battling against each other for the Golden B-Boy award and $100,000 in prize money. As with other reality shows, the bottom two crews each week are asked to perform against each other, and both performances are critiqued by the judges. The viewers at home, however, have the final decision on who gets to stay and which crew has to leave. The departing crew performs one last time before leaving the stage. This cycle continues until one crew emerges successfully from all the challenges and rounds of voting. Challenges can include creating routines for a range of diverse music including songs by Michael Jackson or James Brown, or using a set of randomly assigned props. The show is hosted by Mario Lopez, a contestant on another popular dance show, *Dancing with the Stars*, which is more traditional in the selection of dance forms assigned to contestants. Originally pitched for NBC, the show airs on MTV.

So You Think You Can Dance is another reality dance show, similar in concept, but focusing on the moves of the individual dancer doing routines with partners in various genres of music, with the prizes including a role in Celine Dion's show in Las Vegas as well as cash and the title of "America's Favorite Dancer." Those routines that are often the most popular with audiences are the hip hop or break dancing routines; the show has had six seasons in the United States, and its popularity has created many spinoffs.

Urban dance was also featured in the movie *Save the Last Dance* (2001), which in some ways recycled the ideas of the 1980s films which showed dance as a vehicle for teenage aspirations. The main characters, Sara, a white girl from the Midwest who moves to Chicago,

A performance by Status Quo, one of the groups competing on *America's Best Dance Crew*. (AP Photo/Chris Polk.)

and Derek, a black boy who goes to her new school, find unexpected common ground in their interest in dance. Sara is introduced to hip hop by Derek and incorporates the moves he shows her; her dancing improves as a romantic relationship develops between the two of them. The movie uses a familiar formula: there are lessons in classrooms and abandoned buildings as well as hip hop club scenes. Sara eventually gains admittance to Julliard via a combination of traditional ballet and the style learned from her new friends. *Save the Last Dance 2* (2006) was a straight-to-DVD movie with Sara as the only returning character. The film follows her experiences at Julliard as she continues to struggle between her love of classical ballet and her appreciation for urban dance moves. This focus on urban dance as a legitimate art form by dancers who love movement in general popularized hip hop for a new generation of teenage audiences.

The resurgence of interest in street dance movies and the clash between street and suburbia is brought across clearly in *You Got Served* (2004), in which two friends have to band together to defeat a crew from the suburbs and prove that street dancers are superior. The film also showcases the entanglement with the drug scene and gangs in LA by some of the main characters as they rely on the money they make from selling drugs to enter dance competitions. There are various betrayals including Sonny, a disaffected member of main characters David and Elgin's crew, who defects to their rival Wade's crew, leaking the secret moves that give them a victory in a battle for $5,000. David and Elgin must work through a series of misunderstandings and failures in order to win the prize money in the "Big Bounce" competition sponsored by MTV to pay back Elgin's grandmother, pay off the drug lord, and appear in a Lil' Kim video—securing their reputations as the ultimate dancers. The feuding friends at first decide to create separate crews which divide their talents. Quickly they come to realize this weakens them in competing against the leader of a rival crew of suburban dancers, led by Wade. The slogan "you got served" is exchanged between these battling crews as first one and then the other use it triumphantly when winning battles. The film also featured a cameo appearance by female hip hop artist Lil' Kim. While reviewers criticized the film for its predictable plot, it did secure the number-one slot during opening weekend and garnered interest for the versatility of its dancers. Set in LA, the movie had the requisite elements of dance sequences and romantic complications—David falls in love with Elgin's sister—that would become well known in this subgenre of film, eventually sparking a spate of semi-successful, similarly themed follow-up titles featuring urban and street dance at the core.

Other movies were soon to follow on the success of teenage romantic dance dramas. The *Step Up* (2006) series—the first film, then *Step Up 2: The Streets* (2008), as well as *Step Up 3D* (2010)—are in a sense the continuation of the genre of movies highlighting break dancing. Each features protagonists from the two schools of dance—traditional and street—who must work together in some way with the result being that both their dance styles benefit from cross-pollination of techniques. In *Step It Up*, Nora is a classically trained dancer from the Maryland School of Arts who partners with Tyler, a dancer from the streets, to put together a dazzling senior showcase and secure a job as a professional dancer. In the sequel, Tyler inspires another kid from the streets, this time Andie, who already has a dancing crew, 401, to audition for the Maryland School of Arts dance program. Andie has to choose between her old street crew and the one formed of other people in the arts program who are not traditional dancers; both crews want to compete in the unofficial competition

"The Streets," which is a battle for the title of the best crew. The third release offers the latest in technology with 3D and advanced surround sound technology. The main character, Moose, from the second film in the series, is a dancer but also a student at New York University. Despite his mother's not wanting him to, Moose is drawn into street dancing and a competition with a new crew. The three films share commonalities within the series as well as with the earliest movies featuring street dancing.

The first two movies are set in Baltimore, Maryland, and the latest installment in New York City. The continued focus and emphasis on urban settings is reminiscent of the 1980s films that introduced street dancing into suburban life. Throughout all three films there is an emphasis on the elements that are central to hip hop dance and break dancing; the dancers learn to improvise and test their moves in night clubs and with friends rather than in the practice rooms of their schools with their professional teachers. They design their own routines and impress each other by the versatility, agility, and strength of the various moves they uniquely create. They must work together to beat another

Star Team Varsity, a Japanese dance crew, performs at the World Hip Hop Championship Finals, 2011. (AP Photo/Las Vegas News Bureau, Glenn Pinkerton.)

crew of dancers in order to win a prize or gain entry into the recognized group of dancers. The various films also feature doubting professional choreographers who are won over in the end by the performances of the crews and dancers. Each also features its own love story between the central characters in the film.

In addition to commercially made films, documentaries on b-boys and MCs are also popular. The documentary *Planet B-Boy* (2008) chronicles the global nature of break dancing via the lives of b-boys in France, Japan, South Korea, and the United States as they each try to perfect their dancing as well as win over friends and relatives in their lives who think street dancing is a waste of time, at the same time training for the Battle of the Year competition. Begun in 1990, the Battle of the Year is an example of the contemporary competitions that crews from around the world are involved in, and the film traces the preparations of various b-boys within crews that are preparing for the competition. The Battle of the Year is often referred to as the most difficult competition on the b-boy circuit and has an international audience and participants. Korean b-boy teams have won the coveted title multiple times: Expression in 2002, Gambler in 2004, and Last for One in 2005. These victories are perhaps the reason the city government of Seoul has been funding training for b-boys.

For each of the young men's journeys that the film follows, break dancing is a way to bring meaning and creative expression into their daily lives. The film's emphasis on global interest in break dancing is an indication of its widespread appeal as a form of artistic expression. Johnny Lee, one of the film's executive producers, talks about how the stories told can influence the overall perception of b-boys:

> I want to see the b-boys who dedicate their lives to the art have more roads to individual success and stability. Although b-boying is very popular and highly regarded in Europe and Asia, the majority of Americans just see it as a simple street dance that street kids do. Obviously, this is not the case and projects such as Planet B-boy continue to try to spread the word and culture in the proper light. (Lee)

One of the people the film follows is Ken Swift of the RSC, who is seen advocating and supporting b-boys and the love of breaking. Many of the other key members of the Rock Steady Crew also returned to New York to live and to their roots as the b-boys of the neighborhood, celebrating yearly anniversaries at their adopted park on the corner of 98th Street and Amsterdam. Their commitment to returning to their roots, as well as establishing other chapters of the RSC worldwide, has ensured that the ideals that started b-boying remain preserved for other generations. Many of the founding members, who began breaking as kids and are now adults, including Crazy Legs and Ken Swift, are still actively involved in performing as well as attending events. Ken Swift travels the world as an invited judge to breaking competitions and also has open classes in the Bronx every week during the summer for kids and anyone in the community. He mainly teaches foundation b-boying skills in this class and is still regarded around the world as having some of the world's best foundation skills. The presence of old school breakers on the scene as the original and still active b-boys in the history of hip hop culture gives the RSC crew, and breaking in general, a solid foundation.

Representing the African American tradition of stepping, *Stomp the Yard* (2007) was a popular feature-length film that showcased the footwork and coordinated movements of competitive step teams. The film uses the familiar formula of a love-struck, talented though impoverished protagonist—DJ—who needs to win a dance competition to secure his reputation as a dancer and win the heart of the girl of his dreams. DJ is sent from the gang-run streets of LA to his family in Atlanta after the fatal shooting of his brother, who was also a dancer. While in Georgia, he joins a fictional fraternity and university, and part of his fraternity initiation includes a step routine. Stepping is a particular kind of dance performed in groups similar to the crews of breakers and also in battle-like competitive setting. While he is interested in the step routine the group shows him, he tries to update their repertoire with krumping, a form of street dance created in neighborhoods in LA. The demonstration is met with mixed results as some of the brothers prefer to use the traditional elements of step. The tradition of stepping goes back to the 1940s, when moves were performed in a circle by dancers, and continues to the 1980s and 1990s, when groups would use more complex patterns of movement including crisscrossing rows and pairs of dancers (Fine 6).

Popular among African American fraternities and sororities, stepping involves footwork and all parts of the body to create percussive beats. Occasionally canes and other instruments may be used on stage as well as rhymes, chants, and other vocals. The vocalization makes stepping different from most forms of urban dance. Dancers can call out mottos, their group name, or other message. The roots of step are in a range of African American cultural practices including traditional dance tracing back to the African continent and the Caribbean (Fine 48). In practice, step and its related elements are a form of ritualized dance used to express one's identity as well as group affiliation. The group may often appear in a rigid formation and have more concrete roles and movements than in breaking dancing or other forms of urban dance. Drill and step are related forms of dance which are also used by African American youth to perform and compete in groups (Lacey 5).

In the film, DJ joins the step team just as the group is preparing for the National Step Championship against their campus rivals and all the other high-performing groups in the country. In place of the typical crew rivalry of dance movies, the two fraternities are competing against each other; one of the members of the opposing step team secretly tapes DJ while he is rehearsing. DJ meanwhile participates in the step team in hopes of impressing April, his love interest. But his past comes to haunt him as he is suspended from the university. Through the help of his aunt and April persuading university officials, he is reinstated in time to participate in the final performance at the national competition. The final dance sequence is a dance off between DJ and one dancer from the other semifinalist team. The other dancer goes first, executing all of the steps from the secret video that he has clearly memorized. Not to be outdone, however, DJ performs the same routine but with the addition of a few steps the audience saw his brother perform in the opening dance battle—but this time even more impressive.

Hip Hop Finds a Commercial Groove

In the grand scheme of the development of hip hop culture, the commercial machine was in motion and could not be stopped. Those MCs popular in the scene in the 1970s would soon become the "old school" definition of a hip hop artist as the increasing presence of hip hop music on the radio sparked an interest in both the art and the artists. The transition of MCs from the DJ's sidekick to being the sole focus of a recording happened seemingly by accident. Three unknown rappers for a new label, Sugar Hill Records, recorded the earliest predecessor

on the airwaves in 1979, the single "Rapper's Delight"; these rappers
formed the hip hop group the Sugar Hill Gang. The MCs were still
largely reliant on the work of others, however, as they used live musicians to recreate the melody of a popular song over which they
recorded their rhymes.

"Rapper's Delight" became the song associated with the formal
emergence of hip hop culture and rap music across America, borrowing—or what is known as sampling in the music industry—from
Chic's disco song "Good Times" with an overlaid improvised rap that
was largely unrehearsed:

> I said a hip hop the hippie the hippie
> to the hip hip hop, a you don't stop

Despite being a studio recording, it still had much of the improvisational nature of MCs at hip hop parties encouraging the listeners to
become dancers with references to "let's rock, you don't stop" and
"singin on 'n on 'n on 'n on/the beat don't stop until the break of
dawn." All the early patterns for rap and hip hop as a genre were
unknowingly laid down in this song, including the relationship
between fame and women: "well, my name is known all over the
world/by all the foxy ladies and the pretty girls," as well as the sense
of competition against other MCs: " . . . I'm the grandmaster with the
three MCs that shock the house . . . [against] the sucker MCs try to
prove a point." More than 14 minutes long—quite an unusual length
for a radio song—it included phrases that could be overheard at a block
party including the repeated refrains such as, "di bi di bi, pop the pop
pop you don't dare stop/Come alive y'all and give me what you got"
(quoted in Dimitriadis 184). Relying on the ballad form of poetry,
"Rapper's Delight" was one of the first recordings to represent rap as
oral poetry, relying on a formal structure of rhymes laid over a structure
of beats (Bradley xi). In this sense, rap was borrowing from the musical
tradition of the blues, which also used rhyme schemes and evocative
language. The idea of rap as poetry still has resonance today as 360
the Mack remembers his introduction to creating rap lyrics:

> From what I was told all my life and what still is true, rap music is poetry.
> Just over beats. So what I did was I sat down and I wrote, the only way
> I knew what was poetry to me. The only thing that I was introduced to

as poetry was rap. So I wrote it down as a rap. So when I go to the class, the teacher tells us, everybody has to present it to the class. Mind you this is the first thing that I've done, anything I wrote. So I go up to the class and I'm not gonna speak in poem form, I'm gonna spit it. I'm gonna put some motion into it. And I did. And the class . . . I don't wanna exaggerate but everybody was feeling it. The teacher gave me a A for it. And ever since then, that clicked in my head, like keep writing. You got something going. So it just started off from when I was like 12 and I actually never recorded on a microphone until I was 18. But in between that time I was in high school just freestyling with hip hoppers. (Harkness)

Yet rap's rhyming structure was simplistic, reflecting the still developing nature of the genre. Occurring at the end of each line, the inexperienced MCs did not venture far from the expected flow of beat and rhyme. Taking risks with lyrics to create a distinctive "flow" to the beat of the music was how MCs created a loyal following (Michael Collins 912). Dexterity with rhymes that spoke to the various social and political issues of the day was a hallmark feature of early rap.

Some commemorate this as the moment in which the "MC" label was replaced by "rapper," or someone who began to write rhymes with the beat in mind (Bradley xv). While previously the emphasis had been on supporting the DJ and keeping the party going, the focus now shifted to the MC's ability to showcase his or her verbal dexterity and word play. The precedent for an MC to take center stage with improvised and then rehearsed rhymes was established by "Rapper's Delight" (Cheney 7). The language and music were now working together as the rhythm and beat combined to convey a rehearsed rather than spontaneous message.

Thus the transnational roots of rap, from Jamaican ska and reggae from the 1960s and 1970s would be transformed into the voice of a particular American urban experience (Cheney 11). KRS-One (aka Lawrence Parker) is an artist who is often credited with bringing Jamaican music into hip hop. He would later be an example of how an MC could cross over into film and other media as well as being a well-established artist who held on to social consciousness message in his music. His acknowledgement of the "four corners of hip hop" or the foundation elements of early hip hop culture may have contributed to his interest in the subgenre that would be defined as

"conscious rap" (Smith 3–4). The influence of KRS-One as an alternative to the mainstream commercial product that would soon dominate
the rap genre is evident in underground rapper Visual's reflections on
the group:

> . . . when I started listening to hip hop, it was something normal, it was
> just a different type of music. But made me want to rap, it had to be
> KRS-One, without a doubt. When I heard "My Philosophy", forget about
> it. That's the number one song He gave it a little bit more class and that
> attracted me. His voice was like demanding. So that's definitely the
> man right there and the song that made me say hey, I want to rap, I want
> to write, I want to try to start, I want to do this. This is fun, this looks
> exciting. (Harkness)

The compulsion to try writing rhymes or to try one's best at becoming
a rapper is not undertaken lightly or without the support of others.
Marz is a rapper who remembers his conflicted interest in rap as a
genre when he was a child. "I just started doing it. I made my own studio, at the crib, in the garage, and just started doing it. It's weird
because it's a thing that you just do. I never thought about it, I just
do it. So, it's hard. I never had one point where I was like, okay, I'm
gonna start today to be a rapper or an MC" (Harkness).

Another significant first was also taking place: From the roots of the
Sugar Hill Gang's success would also emerge one of the earliest well-
known disputes over contributor's rights in hip hop recording.
Grandmaster Caz (aka Curtis Fisher, previously Grandmaster
Casanova Fly) was never compensated for the lyrics that he contrib-
uted to "Rapper's Delight" on the basis that his rhymes were lent to
a friend and fellow member of the band the Cold Crush Brothers, Big
Bank Hank (Henry Jackson). Made up of DJ Tony Tone, Charlie
Chase, and Grandmaster Caz, the Cold Crush Brothers were popular
in the late 1970s.

Like many other MCs, Grandmaster Caz got his start as a b-boy
before becoming MC of the group. The Cold Crush Brothers were
rivals to the Fantastic Five, one of the earliest rivalries among hip
hop groups (Fricke and Ahearn vii). Ironically, when the big break into
the recording industry came, it went to Big Bank Hank, as the
Robinsons overhead him rapping to a tape of Grandmaster Caz.
Hank was invited to join the Sugar Hill Gang rather than Caz. Not an

Run-DMC and the Beastie Boys before their Together Forever tour, 1987. (AP Photo/Marty Lederhandler.)

MC at the time but a bouncer, Hank asked his bandmate's permission to use lyrics from his rhyme book. Agreeing on the assumed basis of mutual exchange of professional contacts, this was the last mention Grandmaster Caz would get for his contribution to the first successful rap recording. Grandmaster Caz continues to assert his intellectual property rights to the rhymes to the present day, and this well-known story is one of the earliest of many recording disputes that would follow as artists realized the lucrative nature of the hip hop recording industry. The success of this experimentation by relative unknowns led to early sampling and combination of rock and rap such as Run-DMC's "Walk This Way" with Aerosmith in 1986 and the Fat Boys and Chubby Checker in "Yo, Twist." Rock-inspired rap groups would be a staple of the 1980s with the success of groups such as Run-DMC and the Beastie Boys (Cheney 7).

Sampling was a way to "recycle" various types of African American music by reintroducing parts of jazz, funk, and soul songs into the dance scene. The DJ would manipulate or extract particular tracks and thereby create a new groove. These were used to create rhythm tracks from prerecorded music and recreate sample drum beats, one of the earliest precursors to the rhythms used by MCs to lay their lyrics over. This foregrounding of sound, whereby repetition established the groove of the music, would be a key feature in rap, where the bass drum and vocals combined for rhythmic delivery (Greenwald 267–270).

With the introduction of digital sampling, yet another transition occurred as DJs came to consider themselves producers of songs (Schloss, "Making Beats" 40). No longer reliant on the actual beats in music recorded by other artists, beats could be created or mixed in the recording studio by the DJ himself. Similar to the discovery of two turntables extending the beat by early DJs, digital sampling allowed for the extension and building of longer tracks for those recording in the studio rather than short bursts of improvisational rhymes. From using the music of others to creating track to using sounds to compile their original beats, digital sampling was an important step in the progression of searching for the next beat or set of sounds for MCs to rap over (Schloss, "Making Beats" 38). Sampling also occurred from other parts of African American culture, including the rhymes of children's double-dutch games.

Yet this fun, playful side of rap was soon to get a run for its money from other groups. Run-DMC, another group to come from the urban setting of New York in 1982, this time from the borough of Queens, was made up of Run (aka Joseph Simmons), DMC (aka Darryl McDaniels), and DJ Jam Master Jay (aka Jason Mizell). Only 13 years old at the time, Run was already well known for his ability to work the turntables with quick cuts. Like b-boys before him, rap became an organizing principle for his life as well as those of the other members of his group. Their lyrics often dealt with serious subjects including drug addiction, teen pregnancy, and economic hardship (Dyson and Daulatzai 4).The group was produced by Run's brother, Russell Simmons, who would go on to be a maven of the hip hop recording industry under the label Def Jam Records, which would bring other notable figures onto the scene, including LL Cool J (aka James Todd Smith, also known as Ladies Love Cool James), who signed with the label at the age of 16. LL Cool J would rocket to the status of best-selling artist, establishing both his and the record label's reputation.

Most notably for older brother Russell, who had a history of drug abuse, managing the group became a means of attaining greater social and economic aspirations than his working-class roots could have

Rapper LL Cool J. (AP Photo/Craig Fujii.)

otherwise provided (Brown 89). Russell Simmons would quickly establish himself as one of the earliest hip hop entrepreneurs, later defined as a rap mogul, launching the careers of the key artists in the early years of the genre including Run-DMC, LL Cool J, and the Beastie Boys. Simmons would also use his platform to promote other African American artists by producing the Def Poetry Jam and Def Comedy Jam series on HBO. He also uses his influence to promote activism within the hip hop community, including partnering with MTV on several successive "Get Out the Vote" promotions during presidential election campaigns and serving as chairman of the non-profit group Hip Hop Summit (Peoples 25).

In the early 1980s as everyone was trying out the idea of a rap trio, Run-DMC began with an emphasis on their rhymes and a basic, no-frills style; the group held to a different ideal than that of the nonstop party that would soon dominate hip hop music. They presented a serious image of professional rappers, distinct from the leather and braids of the disco era (Wheeler 213). Helped greatly by MTV showing their first single, "Rock Box," and the first live national rap tour, Fresh Festival, the group was one of the first to brand their confrontational style and aggressive lyrics in the quickly emerging rap scene (Brown 93). With over 20 stops and netting more than $3 million, Run-DMC was the first group to burst onto the national scene. Their success was supported by break dancing crews and the other MCs who toured with them.

Their unique blend of rap and rock was soon in the homes of black and non-black youth around the nation, increasing the genre's visibility and circulation (Dyson and Daulatzai 5). Their bravado was established early on with the success of their first single, "Sucker M.C.s," in 1983:

> And you sucker MC's is who I please
> So take that and move back catch a heart attack

They became one of the first major selling hip hop artists who also had their own unique style, with gold chains, sneakers, track suits, jeans, and hats (Price 183). This pared-down style was in contrast to the flamboyant outfits used by disco artists such as James Brown. Their presence on the hip hop scene quickly translated into mainstream appearances and endorsements; they were the first rappers featured on contemporary mainstream shows that were watched all over the country by a broad demographic including *Saturday Night Live*, *American Bandstand*, and MTV, as well appearing on the cover of key industry magazines including being the first hip hop group to appear on the cover of *Rolling Stone* magazine (Price 184). They were also one of the earliest and most visible examples of compensation disputes in the industry between artists and their managers as they eventually fired their friend and long-time manager Jeff Fludd (Brown 93). Run-DMC inspired many aspiring rappers to take a turn trying their lyrics. Chicago-based rapper Kenny Bogus points to Run-DMC as the group that piqued his interest in rap and rapping: "But when Run DMC and them came out, I think they made a lot of people do it. They brought me into the game. I loved the black leather jackets and the hats. I wanted them. So they really got me to try to put together patterns" (Harkness).

A group who further confirmed the crossover between rock and rap were the Beastie Boys, a trio of Jewish young men who began as a punk group in the early 1980s. Mike D (Michael Diamond), MCA (Adam Nathaniel Yauch), and ad-Rock (Adam Horovitz) made up the final group whose first album, *Licensed to Ill*, was released by Def Jam Records and would sell over five million copies (Price 144). A best seller with over 750,000 copies, the album contained songs such as "Fight for Your Right," which became a teen angst anthem with the chorus, "You gotta fight for your right to party," within the larger message about how parents were hypocrites and fun-killers, asking kids to dress a certain way or keep them from smoking:

> You pop caught you smoking, and he said, "No way!"
> That hypocrite smokes two packs a day

Eventually the Beastie Boys's music reached enough listeners that they opened for Madonna during her 1985 *Like a Virgin* tour as well as for Run-DMC on the *Raising Hell* tour (1986), both of which gave them enough exposure to solidify their status as hip hop artists to be taken seriously (Tanz 87). Trouble was not far away, however, hinting at the problems that would soon plague other well-known hip hop artists, as conflict often flared up at their concerts and female dancers were seen performing in cages. The group would eventually occupy a cult-like status in the hip hop scene, selling in nearly the same volume as Tupac (aka Tupac Amaru Shakur) and Eminem, two of the best-selling artists of the genre. Though the movement from the urban centers onto radios around the nation was gradual, by 1998 rap was outselling any other genre in the music industry (Ogbar, "Hip Hop Revolution" 5).

One of the early duos that would flesh out the difference between the DJ and the MC-turned-rapper was DJ Jazzy Jeff (aka Jeffrey A. Townes) and the Fresh Prince (Willard Christopher Smith Jr.). The two signed a record deal and used a playful style on their first single, "Girls Ain't Nothing but Trouble," to introduce their sound. They used the popular technique of sampling but from an unlikely source: the theme song to the mainstream television show *I Dream of Jeannie*. Using this common referent, they were able to reach a broader, white audience (Saddik 122). They still dealt with relationships with the opposite sex, chasing girls, and the other themes of male rappers, but in a humorous way that camouflaged the violence or sexuality overtly used by others, which was initially chosen by recording companies. Defined by some as "pop rap" because the artists themselves were not from the inner city but the suburbs, they used their lyrics as a way to build upon the shared experiences of youth across class and racial lines (Dyson and Daulatzai 7). For example the warning that

women may not be that easy to manage sexually comes across as one
bemused friend speaking to another in the song's refrain:

>Listen homeboys don't mean to bust your bubble
>but girls of the world ain't nothing but trouble

The interplay between the DJ and his rapper is also captured between
the two:

Jazzy: Yo man you think they see your point
Prince: I don't know I don't think they really do

   At this brief interlude reminiscent of the early interaction between the
DJ and his MC, they are off again with the Fresh Prince telling more
anecdotes about girls welcoming him to their rooms, only to be interrupted by their boyfriends coming home and the Fresh Prince having
to jump out of the window. The emphasis is on the comic retelling of
these failed exploits told mainly by the rapper. Their second album,

DJ Jazzy Jeff (Jeff Townes), left, and the Fresh Prince (Will Smith) at the 1989
American Music Awards. (AP Photo/Lennox McLendon.)

He's the DJ, I'm the Rapper (1998), established the Fresh Prince and his lyrics as the mouthpiece for teenage angst in the late 1990s. It also won the first rap Grammy award (Price 190). Another breakout hit, "Parents Just Don't Understand," captured the imagination of youth around the nation. Again the duo appealed to the universal teenage experience by using lyrics to demonstrate the hardships of being an adolescent with unfeeling parents:

> You know parents are the same
> No matter time nor place

The song goes on to talk about the embarrassing process of buying back-to-school clothes with an entire family and penny-pinching mother—very different from some of the inner-city issues at the core of the artists that were to follow. The contrast between the Fresh Prince's wholesome image and that of the other MCs emerging on the scene, as well as the tumultuous roots of hip hop culture in general, may have poised him as the ideal crossover artist. Smith was soon featured in the popular sitcom *The Fresh Prince of Bel Air*, in which his Philadelphia upbringing was brought into stark contrast with that of his rich California cousins. Running for six seasons, the show established Smith as a likeable actor and provided the launching pad for a string of more than 15 commercially successful films including a mix of action adventure—*Bad Boys* (1995) and *Wild, Wild West* (1999)—as well as comedy—*Hitch* (2005). As his musical career has taken a backseat, his acting has received even more acclaim with two Academy Award nominations for his roles as the boxer Muhammed Ali (2001) and in *The Pursuit of Happyness* (2006).

Perhaps two other extremes of pop rap were MC Hammer (aka Stanley Kirk Burrell) and Sir Mix-a-lot (aka Anthony Ray). Both were known in the 1990s for their party anthems that sold millions of copies and won Grammys, proving that rap could be enjoyed by mainstream audiences. Songs like "U Can't Touch This" by Hammer and "Baby Got Back" by Sir Mix-a-lot are examples of popular dance tunes that came to be identified with a particular moment in the development of hip hop music. "U Can't Touch This" (1990) sampled the popular Rick James song "Superfreak" and reinterpreted it for a new generation looking for a dance anthem (Saddik 122). MC Hammer would become a warning of the mismanagement of a rapper turned

DJ Jazzy Jeff (Jeff Townes) spinning records at Fluid Nightclub in Philadelphia, PA.
(AP Photo/Douglas M. Bovitt.)

millionaire as he declared bankruptcy in the late 1990s. Over time, both MC Hammer and Sir Mix-a-lot would be considered sellouts to the commercial scene rather than rappers of any distinctive talent in comparison with other contemporary artists such as Run-DMC, the Beastie Boys, and DJ Jazzy Jeff and the Fresh Prince.

In their unique way, each expanded how hip hop music would come to focus on rhythm, rhyme, and word play; their lyrics brought together familiar topics of everyday life in unfamiliar ways as a means to engage the listener in their particular vision of the human experience (Bradley xiv). The commercial success and mainstream interest in these early groups paved the way for a generation of creative artists who chose rap as their mode for expression of the marginal experiences of Americans living in society's fringes. Pitch, intonation, accent, cadence, tempo, clarity, and speed were all aspects of a rapper's style, which helped create his unique sound, different from the other artists on the market (Bradley 39).

With the success of "Rapper's Delight," the emphasis in hip hop music shifted from the live experience at a community dance to the individual listener via CD or video. Hip hop culture as a result moved from spontaneous rhymes by MCs to the studio-recorded lyrics of artists (Dimitriadis 179). The previous mix of race and class that contributed to a DJ's or MC's style and his appeal to a particular part of the neighborhood would be replaced by an emphasis on the lyrics and beat themselves. As more women began entering the industry, gender and sexuality were also a part of the elements that distinguished one artist from another. At the center of the new focus was the product: a record rather than the person—the dancer, DJ, or MC. Despite the success of "Rapper's Delight" and other singles, it would still take some convincing before the recording industry and the artists themselves were convinced that hip hop was a viable music form that could make the transition from a popular single to an entire viable album (Brown 93).

As the rap genre continued to gain in popularity, the distinction between commercially popular and socially conscious rap would continue to develop in subgenres of the original hip hop music. Despite being far from the realities of the South Bronx or other underprivileged neighborhoods that gave birth to the hip hop culture, many of hip hop's suburban consumers identified with the search for a voice and the refusal to be silenced. The progression of hip hop from underground subculture to commercially available music is attributed to the popularity of the subgenre defined as "gangsta rap" between 1980 and the mid-1990s. What Tricia Rose calls the "hyper-gangsta-ization" of music, in which rappers focused on violence, sex, and drugs in their videos and lyrics, was accompanied by a spike in record sales (Rose, "Hip Hop Wars" 3). The limited thematic range of commercial rap would come under fire by critics and the general public as gangsta rap narrowed the genre's focus on materialism, sexuality, and violence. Yet the burgeoning rap scene inspired many underground artists when they were young boys, further proving hip hop's attractiveness as a youth culture. Esohel and other rappers from the Chicago underground scene share stories of their introduction to rap in their preteen years:

> Esohel: I would say that since I was 12 I been rhyming, but you don't want to go back to those raps. But seriously, when I was like 15, my freshman year in high school, I jumped in the talent show. . . . my brother had a studio, DJ Poor, had the studio in the attic after school, try to get these dudes to come over. Just write and do our thing. (Harkness)

Esohel discovering rap at the age of 12 and trying out his skills is not unlike the graffiti artist beginning at the age of 11 to experiment with designs and available spray cans. Rap as one element of hip hop that allowed teenagers escape from their conflicts is noted by Verbal Kent:

> Verbal Kent: I used to write rhymes for no reason, just for fun. And that turned into, I think there was a period when I was 17, 18, 19, I was depressed and didn't know what I wanted to do at all, and I loved hip hop and obviously anyone who really loves hip hop for a couple years has to pick up a pen and paper and just be like, "I'm better than you and you can't stop my crew." (Harkness)

The shift in tone from neighborhood block parties and settling differences through dance as opposed to images of gang violence, drugs, and gun culture promoted by commercial hip hop music would sideline the b-boy movement and break dancing in general. The ensuing disillusionment on the part of the founders of hip hop, DJs, b-boys, and MCs alike, would only grow along with the fortunes of those rappers with financial acumen who were able to negotiate the complicated contracts offered by the record industry. A subgenre of rap in the 1980s and early 1990s, gangsta rap would become the vehicle for social expression of a particular black, largely male, experience (Flores 117).

The "hard core" nature of artists, their driving rhythms and social commentary, and their unflinching depiction of the worst aspects of life in the poorest neighborhoods distinguished these musicians and their music from the "pop rap" that was popular in night clubs and parties and more palatable for a mainstream audience. In these songs the "hook" or chorus was often set to a catchy beat and repeated three or more times over the duration of the song. These unflinching glimpses of life in urban centers would be defined as "reality rap." A group of rappers who defined their music as "conscious rap" treated such issues as violence, police brutality, and injustice. The condensation of rap from these various genres into a vehicle that seemed to trigger or inspire violence would soon become part of heated public debate. Originally used to cope with urban frustration and social deprivation, the commercialization of rap and the rise in popularity of gangsta rap would lead many artists to look for alternatives to the mainstream recording industry. These artists formed their own genre, "underground rap," which allowed them to hold to their ideals of socially grounded lyrics unfettered by the demands of popular culture or the pressure of record sales (Smith 2). A mouthpiece from the margins of society to critique discrimination and social disadvantage, rap music and hip hop culture would become one of the defining exports of American popular culture.

The unlikely ways in which rap would be taken up by modern rappers could not have been predicted by those in the studio as the tracks were laid down for "Rapper's Delight." A good example is the story of Hamza Perez, a Puerto Rican self-styled rapper and former gangster who turns to rap as a way to express himself and call those around him out of violence as one member of the hip hop duo M-team. Part of his journey is told in the documentary film *New Muslim Cool*. The film demonstrates how Hamza uses rap and his past as a gangster to reach out to youth who are on the streets in urban Pittsburgh.

Indisputably, however, the genre would be one of the key means by which the margins of America's cities would express the conflicts and contradictions inherent in urban life (Dyson and Daulatzai 6). Over a 20-year period, from 1980 to 2000, rap went from being an underground expression of social and economic disadvantages to a best-selling genre, with rappers winning Grammys and garnering corporate support. As Chuck D, one of the MCs from the reality rap group Public Enemy, would remark, hip hop was "the black CNN," informing both youth and anyone listening about the perils of life in the modern ghetto (Maira 162).

3

Hip Hop Scandals—Sex, Video, and Violence

Used in the early days to keep the crowd engaged and assist the DJ, the master of ceremonies, or MC, began as a partner and helper in the 1970s. As technology developed, however, and the introduction of cassette tapes in clubs became popular, the need for both roles, the DJ and the MC, became limited (Price 36). From the lyrics to the videos, hip hop established itself as a supermacho narrative within which women were assigned a specific, gendered space as maternal "queens" to be respected or sexual beings, "hoes," to be used for pleasure (Ogbar, "Hip Hop Revolution" 77). Women were either money hungry, manipulative, and demanding, or sexually available, without values, self-esteem, or consciousness and at the disposal of male artists. The superiority of men over women would become one of the entrenched themes of the endless hip hop party where dozens of female dancers did little more than provide wriggling backdrops to rap videos. Doubtful at first, the recording industry soon saw the viability of hip hop artists to sell records and of the music to promote a range of commodities from cars to soda. In this transitional period, it was the black male rapper whose swagger and rebellious attitude came to define rap music (Saddik 122).

The late 1980s saw the emphasis in rap music swing towards videos over live performance and the creation of a rapper's persona. Much in the way graffiti writers, DJs, MCs, and b-boys used nicknames, rappers created names and identities for themselves to distinguish one from another in the growing industry (Saddik 117). Accompanying this stage name was often the creation of a persona to validate the image. Playboys, hustlers, pimps, gangsters—the range of figures that MCs chose from were often limited to the urban themes of their music. Some point to the cultural figures of the badman or trickster, present in African American folklore, as contributing to the creation of the modern rap persona (Chang, "Keeping It Real" 548). The aggressive lyrics and swift beats were firmly established regardless of which of the subgenres a rapper was contributing to. A boom in commercially successful male artists further increased this trend in the early 1990s as rap became associated with a "gangster" or urban outlaw who spoke against issues in society related to the black community such as poverty and police brutality. The success of artists in this period crossed over from black and Latino audiences to white suburban youth. Many would feel that these artists had sold out as hip hop was used to sell a range of commodities from burgers to soda, proving that the once alternative genre was now an accepted part of pop culture (Gladney 295).

Rap emerged out of the tradition of black oral rhyming culture, whereby the rapper used metaphors and similes to compare him- or herself to others or to objects in a form of verbal battling similar to that seen previously on the dance floor with b-boys. One of the prevailing metaphors of the genre was that of a neighborhood as a constrictive rather than protective structure where the failure of civil institutions such as the police and education was rampant. Another type of metaphor that was common, metonymy, where a part is substituted for the whole, became emblematic of the materialism rampant in the genre. "Benjamins" for money, "rims" for cars—the metonymy used by rappers would become part of the popular vernacular for youth around the country and eventually the world (Crossley 505). The three major types of rap songs included the boast, where an MC would proclaim his or her prowess; the putdown, where an MC would address the limitations of a challenger or rival; and the message rap featuring social or political commentary (Nelson 18–26). In each of these instances, the MC was setting out his or her unique style as an individual, overlaid by a pervasive self-confident attitude.

This type of bravado and bragging was also seen by other important African American figures at this time including the boxer Muhammad Ali, who was one of the first credited with making bragging a hallmark of his celebrity identity in the public sphere (Perry 58). The bardic or storytelling tradition of black slave culture, expressed as jive talk in the 1960s, was one of the many influences for the rhythm, style, and roots of rap music (Keyes 38). Rappers also employed figurative language to engage the imagination of their listeners, often using images of murder or street violence, for which the genre would come under public scrutiny. Speed, emphasis, and tone each contributed to the overall delivery of the rhymes (Saddik 117). Jokes, phrases from popular culture, references to famous places—all of these were part of the arsenal to assert one's abilities. An MC's ability to manipulate language and employ vivid imagery would set him or her apart from others. Rappers engaged in "wars of position" or verbal instead of physical assaults, similar to the territorial disputes of gangs or competitions between DJs, taggers, and crews in the early days of hip hop (Perry 59), this time not only in their neighborhoods or localities but on the national stage.

A rapper's ability to establish a "flow" or lyrical cadence was essential to creating a reputation and following; the clarity and speed of the rhymes, breath control, and manipulation of the number of syllables to the beats per minute gave each rapper his or her own distinctive voice. The ability to control the beat and the rhyme together was one of the signature talents of those rappers who gained prominence in the 1980s and 1990s as the genre was establishing itself on the radio and television. Now packaged as recorded work as opposed to live performances, the vocal quality of the rapper mattered in distinguishing one's unique sound from that of others. As the most popular artists, including Tupac, Dr. Dre, and Jay-Z, would soon demonstrate, rappers could develop loyal fans that would set music industry sales records. The backgrounds of rappers would also become important to the way that they approached their lyrics. Perhaps one of the most talented lyricists of his time before his death, Tupac was raised by a mother who was a former Black Panther, and he kept his original name instead of using a stage name.

Popularized on *Yo! MTV Raps* and BET's *Rap City*, Ice-T, N.W.A., Easy-E, Dr. Dre (aka Andre Young), Ice Cube (aka O'Shea Jackson), and Snoop Doggy Dogg (aka Calvin Broadus) became household names across America (Dimitriadis 188) as television took the most popular artists and their videos into the homes of middle-class youth in the

1980s and 1990s. The music video quickly came to replace the early days of live battles between MCs; the new emphasis became the visual images used to convey the lyrics of a particular song.

Eventually rap music and rappers would come to represent the contemporary lives of urban, young, black men and circulate limited gender stereotypes for women (Forman 71). Stories of incarceration, injustice, and the failure of civil society for black people—particularly young men—would become recurring themes in the various subcategories of hip hop music including socially conscious and gangsta rap. The gangsta rapper came to occupy the space of an urban hero or modern American rebel for many outside of the neighborhoods in which hip hop originated. But this figure was not without critics, as the lyrics and videos of male artists would come to be synonymous with violence against women and each other (Heath, "Hip Hop Now" 715).

N.W.A. (Niggaz with Attitude) was one of the earliest rap groups from the West Coast to capture the nation's attention and translate this interest into record sales, despite their bleak look into the perils of inner-city life in South Central Los Angeles. The group considered their style "reality rap," and in the same way that MCs from the Bronx were rapping about the challenges facing the youth of New York, N.W.A. became the hard hitters who spoke unflinchingly about the limitations of the criminal justice system for black males (Morgan, "Real Hip Hop" 197). Their lyrics were committed to the unapologetically violent, crude, and harsh expression of a shared anger over racial, social, and economic hardships (Saddik 115). Opinions were divided on whether their insistence on retelling the stories of the destructive forces in their communities and the manner in which they chose to do so, explicit rap, classified them as a negative influence as well.

N.W.A.'s use of profanity led to decreased airtime, which only served to fuel support by their listeners. The founding members were Easy-E (aka Eric Wright), Dr. Dre (aka Andre Young), DJ Yella (aka Antoine Carraby), Ice Cube (O'Shea Jackson), and Arabian Prince (Mik Lezan). Their second album, *Straight Outta Compton* (1988), which also featured MC Ren (Lorenzo Patterson), established them as vocal and somewhat vicious analysts of the inequalities of urban life. Tracks such as "F—k the Police," from their album *Straight Outta Compton* (1988) called attention to tensions based on racism between white police officers and innocent black men, and caused not only alarm but incurred investigation by the FBI (Price 175). The lyrics leave no doubt as to their distrust of the authorities:

> F—k tha police, comin' straight from the underground
> A young nigga got it bad because I'm brown and not the other color

In addition to airing suspicions about flagrant discrimination by civil authorities, the song also established the group and the West Coast as serious contributors to the growing gangsta rap genre. The seething rage expressed by N.W.A. would come to signify the politically conscious element in hip hop music (Martinez 286).

Ice Cube and Dr. Dre would both leave the group in the late 1980s or early 1990s to establish their own successful careers as solo artists, and the group would eventually disband. Dre's *The Chronic* (1992) set the precedent for some the most egregious complaints against the type of rap music that would come to symbolize the hip hop recording industry: celebrating violence, drug culture, and the subjugation of women, albeit with innovative lyrics set to a percussive beat. Dre's album was named after the slang term for marijuana used in Southern California, further defining the West Coast nature of his music. The commercial viability of Dre and Ice Cube would widen the gap between hip hop's origins as spontaneous creativity and the entrepreneurial machine that would become the rap music industry. They had left a firm imprint on the early days of rap as a genre to express the reality and frustration of those living in some of America's most downtrodden inner cities. Dr. Dre's Death Row Records (cofounded with Suge Knight) would produce some of the biggest names in hip hop including Snoop Dogg, Eminem, and 50 Cent, among others.

Soon to follow, also in 1988, was the launch of the first hip hop magazine by students at Harvard, *The Source*, a publication that would go on to be one of the founding publications about the now established hip hop culture. Many of these rappers, including Ice Cube and Snoop Dogg, would again cross over into film and television as their popularity as celebrities grew in the late 1990s, further cementing the idea that hip hop was here to stay as a cultural force.

Rappers as Gangstas

Yet while rap and rap artists demonstrated commercial viability, the depictions of violence, and the violent acts among artists themselves,

Rapper Snoop Dogg performs at the 10th annual ESPY awards. (AP Photo/Mark J. Terrill.)

threw a growing shadow over the hip hop industry and raised questions about inner city and black culture. Regional divisions were soon to emerge, and artists were increasingly likely to identify themselves as East Coast or West Coast rappers or from the "Dirty South." West Coast artists such as Dr. Dre, Ice Cube, Snoop Doggy Dogg, and Tupac were outselling their East Coast contemporaries (Ogbar, "Hip Hop Revolution" 110). Some of this difference could be attributed to the different focus of the artists themselves; West Coast rappers were generally accused of promoting a hip hop that was purely pleasure seeking and party centered. With lyrics that featured sexual exploits, violent gang encounters, and the pursuit of materialism, West Coast rap gained a distinctive macho flavor. Rappers on the East Coast, on the other hand, were engaged with the social and political challenges facing black youth, including the promotion of sexualized gender stereotypes and the unequal distribution of resources (Cheney 100).

The commercialization of hip hop and the popularity of the West Coast artists further fueled the division between these two styles as gangsta rap became the dominant genre in terms of record sales and distribution. In either case, the effect was the same: rap became a window on urban culture but a particular interpretation of it that included materialism, scantily clad women, and gun culture (Rose, 1994, 135). There were figures that became emblematic of this genre across artists, including those of the thug, the hustler, the gangster, and the pimp (Rose, 2008, 3), and the rampant materialism sought by them became a defining element of commercial hip hop which grew in popularity thorough the promotion of the recording industry. The lessons were obvious and well learned by later East Coast artists such as Jay-Z (aka Shawn Carter), DMX, and Nas, who adopted the gangsta style and also achieved commercial success (Ogbar, "Hip Hop Revolution" 11). Particularly in 1992 through1995, gangsta rap promoted not only rampant materialism but also the glorification of organized crime, with rappers posing as the pimp/Mafioso/drug lord. Featuring urban violence such as the drive-by shootings, the idea of an "urban solider" was at the center of most rap songs with a fierce emphasis on the individual over the community (Ogbar, "Slouching toward Bork" 168).

The image of the pimp, or materially successfully MC, began to dominate videos and lyrics of popular artists over some of the analysis of social injustice or abuse taken up by early artists. Snoop's first album, *Doggystyle* (1993), and the resulting multi-platinum record sales helped establish gangsta rap as a genre of hip hop (Price 186). "Gin and Juice," one of the emblematic tracks from his debut album, became a popular party and club song that represented a growing interest in the hip hop party scene. He unapologetically referred to drinking, sex, and drugs while scantily clad women proliferated in the scenes of his videos. Snoop's popularity soon established the commercialized hip hop thrill-seeking scene:

> Two in the mornin and the party's still jumpin
> cause my momma ain't home

The hypersexualized drive of the male artist became a staple of rap music as well as the assumption that there would always be an abundance of available women or "hoes" for entertainment. Snoop's popularity as a hip hop icon translated into film appearances, including *Training Day* (2001) and *Soul Plane* (2004).

By the 1990s, the fan base for hip hop, about 70 percent white Americans, affirmed the tales of woe from the inner city over the messages about social inequalities that criticized white people. The controversy within the hip hop community among artists is similar to the challenges that faced break dancing as it caught the attention of the public at large. Rappers were increasingly drawn into one of two categories: "keeping it real" or "pop hip hop," which was seen to compromise hip hop's sociopolitical message in order to sell records. In contemporary pop music, hip hop songs are at least a third of the major hits on Billboard's top-40 charts (Tanz 75).

In videos such as "Fantastic Voyage" by Coolio in 1994, the rap scene became one big, continuous party with men entertaining themselves as women looked on or provided the entertainment (Grant 19). The chorus and the video depict the rapper and his friends in a sedan barely driving down the block because the music is bouncing them all up and down so hard:

> Come along and ride on a fantastic voyage
> slide slide slippity-slide

There are serious moments buried throughout the song which allude to why the fantastic voyage is a kind of escape from the realities of the violence and betrayal of inner city life. The references to drive-bys and gangs are sandwiched between the calls to climb aboard on the endless party car. But Coolio was not alone in promoting this escapist rap, which simultaneously acknowledged the perils of urban life as well as promoted a nonstop party with lascivious women as one of the potential rewards of living so close to danger. In popular videos by Warren G and Nate Dogg, such as "Regulators," the scene is set for a night of womanizing but interrupted by threats of violence. The carjacking and mugging take place in front of "skirts" or "hookers," thereby confirming the two main staples of a gangsta rapper's life: women and guns.

> It was a clear black night, a clear white moon
> Warren G was on the streets, trying to consume

Nate Dogg sympathizes with his "homey" Warren G, whose rings, necklace, and other jewelry are taken from him at gunpoint, and Nate arrives in the nick of time to make sure that the muggers regret their actions. The implicit violence of "bodies turn[ing] cold" and the link between Nate Dogg and Warren G exemplify the kind of bravado that characterized gangsta rap. Yet, maintaining the tension between the rappers' twin tendencies towards violence and rampant masculine sexuality, the duo turn their attention back to the waiting and willing women, even as they shoot their assailants. With revenge securely established, the rest of the night is reserved for "freak mode" with the "skirts" who have just had a firsthand display of the duo's ability to regulate against any infringement of their person or property.

Other artists would shift even further away from violent references and rely solely on the idea of life as a nonstop party with women constantly at hand as part of a sexual buffet. In Snoop's "Gin and Juice" women featured prominently as dancers or extras in large crowd scenes, which mimicked house parties. The function of these female dancers was largely as "video hoes," or young, highly sexualized groupies who were at the mercy of the male vocalists and were objects for their pleasure (Emerson 116). The implication was that sex was not between consenting partners but defined by a power relationship where men could use violence to discipline misbehaving or unwilling women by force or humiliation (Adams and Fuller 950). When mentioned in songs by male rappers, women were given demeaning titles rather than referred to by name: "hoe," "chickenhead," or worse became the call symbols for females in both videos and lyrics.

Race and Rap

The success of Snoop Dogg, Dr. Dre, and other artists gave rap and hip hop culture a largely masculine African American context and culture. Their autobiographical experiences with drugs, gangs, and the inner city lent them an authenticity that defined the early years of gangsta rap and fueled debates about whether rap represented the violence of urban life or created it (Condry 639). The popularity of the genre among white, suburban youth could not have been predicted, but beginning in the 1980s, white listeners from Generation X responded to the counter-culture message of rap as a means of dealing with their own teenage angst (Kitwana 26). Soon to follow were white artists who attempted to cross into the rap genre with varying degrees of success, the precursor being the success of the Beastie Boys. One of the earliest white rappers was Vanilla Ice (aka Robert Van Winkel), whose career eventually faded after a few popular singles that despite selling well did not meet the criteria for deft lyrics or good beats. In addition, Vanilla Ice's modest upbringing in the suburbs of Texas—and a few misleading tales about hardships suffered in childhood that were uncovered as fabrications—kept him from the sort of street credit that rappers needed; he wasn't seen as authentic but rather as someone posing (Boyd 124).

Perhaps one of the biggest artists in rap music and the most surprising because of his whiteness has been Eminem (aka Marshall Mathers III). Raised by his mother in the poverty-stricken areas of Detroit, Michigan, and abandoned by his father at an early age, Em, as he is also known, had childhood roots similar to the urban blight experienced by his African American counterparts, and there was no need to pretend to create authenticity. His lyrics would connect to the dislocation from mainstream society expressed by the most popular black

Rapper Eminem performs at Radio City Music Hall during the 2000 MTV Video Music Awards. (AP Photo/Suzanne Plunkett.)

male artists (Als and Turner xvi). His first recording, *The Slim Shady LP* (1999), was backed by Dr. Dre, his producer, whose own reputation in the industry lent credence to Em's work (Boyd 127).

Instead of foregrounding gang violence, he talked about being left by his father in childhood, living on welfare, and feeling out of place in high school. His themes were of general teenage angst, ones that other white kids who had never seen similar hardships could nonetheless relate to. Eminem managed to win over the other side of the hip hop community as well; this he did this with complex rhymes that established him as talented despite being white. Grudging endorsements came from across the hip hop community including institutions such as *The Source* magazine. Em defined his own style and in some cases broke major industry taboos for rappers, such as insulting his mother, which surprised many of his counterparts. The rage expressed by Eminem against his mother, ex-wife, and society would be his defining feature, and his listeners were quick to identify with him. His *Marshall Mathers* record sold five million copies in the first month, making it the fastest-selling hip hop album of all time (Elrick 7).

The highest praise given to Eminem was from an unexpected and unlikely source—UK poet and Nobel laureate Seamus Heaney, who was also a former professor of poetry at Oxford University. During an interview in 2003, when asked who was using lyrics in an innovative way in comparison to musical greats such as Bob Dylan and John Lennon, Heaney pointed out Eminem as someone who had influence on his entire generation. The comments surprised nearly everyone, including Heaney's son, who was also a musician. But they are an example of the way the controversy behind Em's rhymes do not limit people's appreciation of his style and wit.

East Coast versus West Coast Feuds

The rifts that opened up between rappers on both coasts were fueled by the bravado and need to establish the reputation of rappers. The hip hop culture that originated on the East Coast was being modified and responded to by MCs, dancers, and DJs from urban centers on the West Coast. The introduction of new groups and sounds from West Coast urban centers such as Los Angeles took hip hop in new directions. The perceived differences in regional style were fueled by the competitive nature of hip hop culture, rooted in the battles for excellence of early MCs (Perry 156). The West Coast, perhaps best represented by Dr. Dre and Snoop Dogg, was often responded to by Jay-Z and Notorious B.I.G. (aka Christopher Wallace or Biggie Smallz) from the East Coast. Many felt that these disputes were scripted or contrived in order to boost a sense of rivalry and thereby record sales for new titles. In either case, both sides presented unflinching views of the complex gender relationships in urban America including infidelity and single parenthood; these views were sometimes taken to be accurate reflections of African American life rather than one interpretation of a population's experience (Dyson and Daulatzai 137).

The rivalries were often taken into the mainstream media via videos and interviews such as Snoop's "New York, New York," which shows him marching through Manhattan stepping on buildings. The trash talking between artists such as 50 Cent and Ja Rule became a regular staple of the noted rivalry between the groups. Yet the violent deaths of Tupac in 1996 and Notorious B.I.G. in 1997 were reminders that the gang roots of hip hop artists were not necessarily media inventions.

A third "coast" emerged in the 1990s, the "Dirty South," with the rising popularity of Southern rappers including Outkast, Arrested Development, and Kanye West. Though 2 Live Crew had set a precedent for the continuous Southern party, the later artists would make it their own.

Rappers and Video Hoes

In much of the music and many of the videos, women were often sexualized as onlookers at the party—highly visible but only as bodies. These were usually scantily clad young Latino or black women in the dozens, clustered around the rapper and his friends and never engaged directly with the camera either in speech or gaze, thereby existing only as objects for the rapper, his friends, and the viewer's enjoyment. The opposite extreme of these "honeys" always ready for a party was the hardworking matriarch, either mother or grandmother, entirely absent from the musical scene as sacrosanct subjects not to be messed with. Other variations on these stereotypes included the unwed teenage mother living on welfare. Groups such as N.W.A. were characterized by their references to violence; conversely 2 Live Crew entered the scene in 1989 with explicitly sexual lyrics and unapologetic album titles including that of their third release, *As Nasty As They Want to Be.*

The group began as many others in the early trends of hip hop with a DJ, Mr. Mixx (aka David Hobbs), and two rappers, Fresh Kid Ice (aka Chris Wong Won) and Amazing Vee (aka Yuri Vielot). However, they would quickly establish themselves as one of the lightening rod groups of the late 1980s and early 1990s from their very first album. They could not be accused of overstatement, as many of their songs could not be played on the radio, including "Me So Horny," which pushed the outer limits of previous rap songs and shocked many with its blatant sexual references. The chorus of the song was two repeated phrases: "Me so horny/Me love you long time" with a woman moaning in the background. The group and the album would be the first to be prosecuted and found guilty under obscenity charges in Florida in 1990.

However, these charges were eventually overturned in a growing debate over free speech and media autonomy. Despite the controversy, the album sold over three million copies—this even though it was banned for sale in some states, such as Florida, and many retailers were arrested for selling the album to undercover police officers. The unlikely defender of the group, professor Henry Louis Gates Jr., testified that their lyrics had roots in African American slave tradition and their rights should be protected. The Supreme Court agreed and overturned the decision of the Florida district court. The scuffle over 2 Live Crew was just one example of the divided opinions of the general public on rap music; yet records kept selling, encouraging more artists to consider taking up the microphone. 2 Live Crew continued to release other songs that spoke plainly about sex, and their album covers featured women in skimpy bathing suits. The idea of a "ho" or woman who was at the ready for sexual liaisons also came to represent an insult to another man's—even a rapper's—masculinity. A "ho" came to embody the antithesis of the gangsta or the "g" that was the hypermasculine version of the rapper. The motto during this period and one of the anthems of gangsta rap could be summarized as "g's up, hoes down."

Concern over the violence, sexuality, and misogynistic messages prevalent in gangsta rap did not go unchecked, however, as interest groups such as Empower America and the National Congress of Black Women, as well as members of Congress, called on the record industry to clean up the radio airways. Time Warner, at the time with a 50 percent ownership in Interscope Records, one of the primary producers of gangsta rap, caved in to public scrutiny and sold its shares. The public outcry against such depictions of womanhood was countered by the volume of record sales since by 1998: rap outsold any other musical genre (Ogbar, "Hip Hop Revolution" 5). Critics of the various genres of hip hop began to raise questions of how women were depicted as either sexualized objects or recipients of violence.

In 2004, another large-scale controversy emerged over a video of rapper Nelly (aka Cornell Hayes) which featured much of the standard fare of rap videos: women dancing provocatively, blissfully ignoring the men rapping around them. What set Nelly's "Tip Drill" (2004) video apart from the garden-variety hip hop party, however, was the moment when the rapper slides a credit card between the buttocks of a dancer (Reid-Brinkley 237). The students of the women's college Spelman canceled a campus community service activity that would have featured an appearance by the rapper to benefit his 4Sho4Kids Foundation to show their outrage at this particular video but also at the gender stereotypes in hip hop music. The high-profile nature of a historically black college withdrawing support for a multimillion dollar artist was too juicy for the media to ignore: the controversy sparked *Essence* magazine to kick off the "Take Back the Music" campaign to talk about the representation of women in hip hop.

Yet since the early days of hip hop, women had been a positive part of the industry as performers, managers, or producers. From Kool Herc's sister to Sylvia Robinson of Sugar Hill Records and Kool Lady Blue, the contribution of women was often sidelined along those of the men they promoted or worked with. Female artists such as Queen Latifah and groups such as Salt-N-Pepa began to respond to the commodification and commercialization of the images of women in hip hop culture in a woman-centered voice and with women-centered themes, reinterpreting hip hop and rap for both male and female artists (Patricia Collins 15). They were the among the first female rappers to take center stage not as the objects of male desire but as desiring beings themselves, with frank lyrics about the problems in male-female relationships and their attitudes towards sex and sexuality (Perry 154). Following in the lyrical dissent of teenager Roxanne Shante, female MCs would bring onto the airwaves their experiences. In this sense they brought the "wreck" into the genre because in many senses they had to dispel the image of the silent and sexy video vixen rampant in the work of their male counterparts. They claimed a public voice for black women in the public sphere (Carpenter 808–809).

Rather than being feminine objects being spoken about, female rappers put themselves, and their needs and goals, squarely in the center of their songs and videos. They introduced positive images of black women into the public sphere which had previously been missing in the work of male artists; their accompanying commercial success was proof that women-centered themes in hip hop culture were much needed.

4

Make Room for the Ladies

The earliest feminist responses to male rappers were female MCs who responded to the supermachismo inherent in the largely male environment by stepping to the microphone under their own steam to introduce women-centered topics and images. In the case of the first wave of female rappers, their videos and lyrics varied drastically from those of their male colleagues. By taking to the microphone, they contested the images of women as passive, sexualized beings in the videos and music of their male counterparts. They entered the scene with active and aggressive lyrics, willing to tackle the deficiencies in male-female relationships in an open and honest manner. Protests against violence against women, gender inequality, and sexual dependence became staples of the first wave of female rappers with a feminist consciousness (Emerson 126). Female rappers in the underground were focused on a similar mission: to challenge the depiction of women by a male dominated genre. They used the same system that depicts women as promiscuous, vapid, and conniving to present their versions of women as thinking, feeling, powerful beings. In some ways, women artists were better poised to enter into hip hop music because they already had topics such as domestic abuse to talk about in their music. Many contemporary MCs believe that meaningful content can increase the impact of lyrics on the listener:

Marz: You got to have something to say. . . . It's more than being a rapper. You have to have some type of evaluation and psychology in life and be able to put it in a way that people can relate to and hopefully teaches 'em something. Not necessarily teaches 'em but adds something to 'em. That's what makes a good MC. Where you leave from listening to the track or watching a live show, it just leaves you bigger than you were before you heard it. (Harkness)

In the 1990s the women rappers who took to the stage often represented themselves in masculine dress and speech in order to compete in the masculine-defined space of rap music and have attention paid to the message behind their music. In a genre that focused on violence and power, early female artists avoided the sexually attractive marketing that would take over the industry. These two periods can be thought of as the early MC in the 1990s and the sexy female MC who emerged in 2000. In both cases, these artists and groups were making conscious choices to give voice to their experiences over being victims or objects in the videos and music of their male counterparts (Perry 162). Their presence in the hip hop scene and commercial success opened new channels to address the sexism circulated by the industry (Perry 168) and address the limitations of male depictions of black womanhood. Female artists were known to make use of the "dis" song whose purpose was to disrespect or refute the lyrics of another known recording. "Dis" tracks or responses became a tradition in the genre where an MC could respond to an insult, address someone too prideful, or establish superiority over another (Phillips, Reddick-Morgan, and Stephens 262). By their dress, speech, and actions, female rappers responded to the depiction of women in gangsta rap by confronting it directly in some cases and calling for female solidarity in others.

One of the earliest and most successful examples of a "dis" was by a teenager, Roxanne Shante, 14 years old in 1984 and one of the first female voices to be heard on the radio. With a father who was a music producer, Roxanne recorded "Roxanne's Revenge" in response to the male group UFTO's "Roxanne, Roxanne" in which the group complained about the lack of interest in them by a neighborhood beauty, Roxanne, despite their best efforts. This vehement response by a young girl would become one of the earliest and most famous examples of a "dis" song and of the reframing of masculine perceptions of women by a female MC (Perkins 57). Shante's version would be one of dozens but remains the most popular response to UFTO and began what many now refer to as the "Roxanne wars" (Hobson and Bartlow 4).

Sha-Rock (aka Sharon Jackson) was the only female rapper in the group the Funky Four + 1 More (1976). Still in high school, she demonstrated that getting started early as an MC was just as potent for teenage girls as it was for teenage boys living in the inner city to gain a sense of agency, empowerment, and self-expression. She would later join Lisa Lee and Debbie Dee's group, Us Girls, the first female rap group to get any radio time (Ogbar, "Hip Hop Revolution" 78). They appeared in the 1980s film *Beat Street*, performing their single "Us Girls Can Boogie Too," a woman-empowering anthem. Sha-Rock came to define the "old school" female MC at a time when most of the attention was going to male performers. She made many of her early appearances at DJ Kool Herc's parties (Philips, Reddick-Morgan, and Stephens 255).

At first the difference between these self-promoted female artists and their male counterparts was not entirely clear; they bragged and grabbed their crotches in the style of male MCs because miniskirts and heels were considered constraining and too womanly. They replicated the aggressive attitude of the males in the genre. As male rappers became more commercialized, however, a growing response could be seen in the emergence of popular female artists who expressed their sexuality, identity, and daily struggles in unique videos, lyrics, dance, and dress (Emerson 115). The increasing presence of strong, independent female voices, which were also commercially successful and impressive to recording studios, helped create a response to the male-dominated arena of gangsta rap which were monopolizing the genre. Women artists began to reclaim the image of black women in the music and videos of male rappers. Their ability to speak for themselves allowed them to express a feminist agency or sense of self missing from the lyrics and images promoted by male artists. Female artists contradicted the idea that black women were either sexy playthings or downtrodden mothers. But the marketing of these artists would reflect a trend in the industry from strong, female voices that were masculine or androgynous in dress towards artists who tended towards the explicitly sexual (Cheney 8).

In the late 1980s and early 1990s however, female artists such as Queen Latifah, Salt-N-Pepa, Lauryn Hill, and Eve emerged on the hip hop music scene to challenge the limitations of misogynist lyrics and assumptions about black womanhood with their lyrics which directly addressed issues facing black women (Ogbar, "Hip Hop Revolution" 90). Coinciding with what some call the "Golden Age of

Hip Hop" (1987–1994), they came onto the scene as independent, active, and dynamic performers, proving that female artists could not only sell records but also use their lyrics to bring women's causes, goals, and issues to the forefront (Pough 98). Singing and rapping as themselves, as real women and not the idealized girls in rap videos, they challenged the misrepresentations of women in rap music.

Salt-N-Pepa, arguably one of the most important female groups in the history of the genre, began as a group of three African American women who were brash, cool, and vicious in their lyrics, dance moves, and appearance. Characterized from the beginning by their attitude-infused lyrics, they were unabashedly strong women who presented some of the first women-centered messages in hip hop culture with a distinctively black, female attitude (Perry 171). With a longevity not enjoyed by many other female rap groups, Salt-N-Pepa became the signature female voices of the first wave of female artists. In 1987 with their first album, boldly titled *Hot, Cool, and Vicious*, they unapologetically introduced to the hip hop industry a unique blend of sexually assertive, socially aware, and catchy lyrics. The group was composed of Cheryl James as "Salt," Sandra Denton as "Pepa," and Deidra Roper as the DJ Spinderella (who replaced their original DJ, Latoya Hanson). They promoted their sexuality in a frank and empowering voice, using their friendships with their DJ and other female groups to promote a positive image of black womanhood. They purposefully responded to the images and notions of women circulated by male artists, including an answer track, "The Showstopper," in 1985 under their previous name, Supernature, in response to hit single "The Show Stoppa (Is Stupid Fresh)" by Doug E. Fresh and Slick Rick (Phillips, Reddick-Morgan, and Stephens 257).

Their major hits were frankly sexual and their dress masculine, but both were expressions of their unique style rather than mimicking that of male artists. They enjoyed a decade of high-profile success in their uniquely themed videos and consistent platinum album sales (Price 185). "Push It" was their break-out hit from the first album in 1987, in which they spoke directly about their sexual preferences and called other women to do the same:

> Salt and Pepa's here, and we're in effect
> Want you to push it, babe

Rap group Salt N' Pepa performs at the 17th annual Grammy Awards, 1995. (AP Photo/Reed Saxon.)

The chorus left little to the imagination, as did the MCs' moves in concert and in the video: "Ah, push it—push it good/Ah, push it—push it real good." The meteoric rise of "Push It" on the charts was followed by moderate success of a second album. Their third, *Blacks' Magic* (1990), featured "Let's Talk about Sex" (1990), an even franker semipolitical discussion of sleeping around, STDs, and other behaviors associated with the hip hop party scene and youth culture in general in the early 1990s. They sold singles again in record numbers at a time when the myth of AIDS as a purely homosexual disease was being dispelled. Talking about sex and AIDS in such an open and frank manner established them as a group with a social consciousness reminiscent of the early days of hip hop music. A related version of the song, "Let's Talk about AIDS," appeared soon after and directly addressed the reality of transmitting AIDS, thereby further establishing the group's willingness to respond to social issues critical to their fans' well-being. At the start of the original song, the two MCs discuss the taboos they are about to break:

> Yo, I don't think we should talk about this
> Come on, why not?

As with "Push It," the chorus could not have been franker. The group continued to mature and expand both their message as well as their appeal on the hip hop scene with their fourth album, *Very Necessary*.

The popular single "Whatta Man" (1993), in collaboration with the R&B group En Vogue, talked about issues such as sexual responsibility and egalitarian relationships (Ogbar, "Hip Hop Revolution" 81). This type of cross-genre work was an example of how female artists created their own community in order to promote women's solidarity as they expressed a shared understanding of women's feelings and aspirations. In the "Whatta Man" video, the roles were reversed in that heavily muscled and bare-chested men were pursued by women clearly interested in pursuing them for pleasure on their own terms. The men in the video are not mere replicas of the bimbos in videos by male artists: rather they enjoy the pursuit by these dynamic and attractive women. The impression is one of mutual consent and pleasure rather than the domination of one gender over the other (Emerson 132).

The song featured strong female voices rapping about a good man who was faithful and funny, and it was a marked departure from the sexually focused lyrics of the group's contemporary male artists. It showed that female black rappers were prepared for interpersonal relationships between men and women in a way that male rappers had not previously been. In discussing their ideal man, they both celebrate him and also hold up an example for their male counterparts:

> I wanna take a minute or two, and give much respect due
> To the man that's made a difference in my world

The video, which featured the group in glamorous gear as opposed to their traditional baggy pants and masculine outfits, proved their versatility and ability to keep up with their high-fashion collaborators. The chorus left no doubt as to the happy, satisfied state of these women with their men.

The group's video for "Shoop" was also a rare reversal in women singing about men in sexual terms with good-looking, half-dressed male dancers serving as the "eye candy" or "video hoes" (Grant 19). The lyrics are an unabashed exploration of women's interest in men, checking them out, picking them up, and sharing their sexual exploits in much the same way that male MCs had been talking about women since before "Rapper's Delight." From the first notice to the approach, their lyrics left nothing to the imagination. In the song, the group acknowledges that this forwardness from a woman may be classified as inappropriate or that others may misunderstand the type of behavior towards men that takes the initiative. At the same time they discuss their desire, they simultaneously explain that there is nothing wrong with an assertive woman taking what she wants and behaving how she wants within the context of interest in the opposite sex. This expressive sexuality was a signature feature of Salt-N-Pepa as one of the first female rap groups in the early 1990s to take to the stage and unapologetically reframe the way women were seen and heard in hip hop culture. While some would criticize the group's later collaborations or lyrics as too mainstream, their influence on hip hop and their legacy for other female artists is undeniable.

The baggy pants and mostly masculine image Salt-N-Pepa chose would contrast with artists who marketed themselves differently, such as Lil' Kim and Foxy Brown, performers who chose to dramatically showcase their femininity with hypersexual dress. Other notable contemporary female rappers who also chose a confident rather than purely sexual tone included MC Lyte (aka Lana Michele Moorer) whose single "Ruffneck" was the first by a female solo artist to sell enough copies to reach gold status (Ogbar, "Hip Hop Revolution" 81). MC Lyte's style was more masculine, with gold chains, sweat pants, and often no make-up, to accompany her raspy, low voice. Her assertive lyrics challenge others to defy her. MC Lyte follows the Salt-N-Pepa style of describing in detail the masculinity that she finds appealing:

> I need a ruffneck
> I need a man that don't stitch like a bitch

She calls for unity between herself and her man, rather than the one-night partying stand that male artists were referring to in their lyrics. Sex, however, and her partner's sexual prowess are not far from her mind, nor is his ability to give pleasure. MC Lyte was a voice in between the assertive style used by early hip hop female artists and the hypersexualized lyrics to come from female artists unafraid to exploit their appeal in order to sell records.

Queen Latifah (aka Dana Elaine Owens) was the first major solo female rap star and is commonly referred to as the 'first lady' of hip hop (Price 178). Her childhood Arabic nickname would become part of her artist's persona. Her journey into music exemplifies the lasting contributions of the three early hip hop leaders, the DJs of the Bronx. Afrika Bambaataa's community group, Native Tongues, was where she recorded her first demo that led to a record deal (Price 178). Her break out single "Ladies First" from her first album *All Hail the Queen*, released in 1989, promoted style and elegance for female artists in addition to being a call for all female MCs to promote a positive image of women (Ogbar, "Hip Hop Revolution" 82). The song was one of the earliest and most clearly articulated feminist messages in hip hop, calling attention to sexism and gender discrimination in the dominant language and images used to refer to black women. She and her fellow MC, Monie Love, throw the rhymes back and forth to each other in a sparring style reminiscent of early hip hop:

> [Monie Love] My sister, can I get some?
> [Queen Latifah] Sure, Monie Love, grab the mic and get dumb

The message at the core of the various stanzas is one of empowerment not just for all women, though it is that, or for female MCs, though it is that as well, but for this particular MC herself. Offering herself up as "a perfect specimen" is an example of bravado used by male MCs to establish themselves as the best or to distinguish themselves from others. The "Ladies First" single would later be listed as one of the 500 most influential songs that shaped rock 'n' roll. The video depicted contemporary female black leaders such as Winnie Mandela and historical figures such as Sojourner Truth as a tribute to women's activities around the world.

From New Jersey but educated in Queens, Queen Latifah's follow up, "U.N.I.T.Y.," was a clear message against misogynistic expressions and a call for unity among female MCs and male supporters, including other rap artists. Qualifying as a "dis" song, Queen Latifah called out men who used words like *bitch* to refer to women. The song challenged the suspect lyrics of other rap songs in which men and women were unfaithful or treated their partners badly by talking instead about love between black men and women, as well as calling to task those who used misogynistic labels for women (Ogbar, "Hip Hop Revolution" 83).

> Every time I hear a brother call a girl a bitch or a ho
> Trying to make a sister feel low

Her call is for men to respect women not as playthings for pleasure or entertainment but as brothers and sisters. She explains what happens when these rules of mutual respect are not followed. She neither wants to be treated as a sex object nor dismissed as a bitch; both are clear in the song as well as the idea that love, rather than lust, between black men and women should prevail: "U.N.I.T.Y., love a black man from infinity to infinity / U.N.I.T.Y., Love a black woman from infinity to infinity." She used her lyrics to address the harmful language and images of women in rap music used by some artists. In the early 1990s, she began to experiment as a media crossover artist with a lead role in a television series, *Living Single* (1993–1998), and then in feature films including *Beauty Shop* (2005); she was the only female hip hop artist to be nominated for an Academy Award for her role in the best picture of that year, *Chicago* (2002).

The consensus among female artists was not one of complete solidarity, however, as rappers such as Lil' Kim (Kimberly Denise Jones) and Foxy Brown (Inga Marchand) came onto the scene in 1996 expressing overt sexuality in their dress and lyrics (Ogbar, "Hip Hop Revolution" 85). Both Lil' Kim and Foxy Brown are perhaps extreme examples of the stereotypical sexual temptress who is also not afraid of violence. Critics point to the launching of these and other hypersexual artists by male producers, pointing to their images as attractive to male sensibilities; in one sense their vixen personas are the female equivalent to those used by the male artists (Michael Collins 937). This list of male promoters and sexualized female artists reads very differently from that of the first wave of female rappers such as MC Lyte and Queen Latifah. The Junior M.A.F.I.A. introduced Lil' Kim, and Jay-Z's record label brought Foxy Brown onto the scene (Philips, Reddick-Morgan, and Stephens 258).

Female rapper Lil' Kim performs at Radio City Music Hall during the 1997 MTV Video Music Awards. (AP Photo/Adam Nadel.)

Lil' Kim and Foxy Brown represented another interpretation of women talking about sex and desire than the approach used by Salt-N-Pepa or Queen Latifah. By using a mixture of blatantly sexual self-representation, imagery on videos, and unapologetic lyrics, these later female artists expanded a purely sexual space unprecedented for female rappers in the hip hop scene (Perry 181). They are known for being frankly and unapologetically sexual, playing up their physical attractiveness rather than minimizing it in the tradition of the first wave of female rappers. The debate on whether this type of marketing was chosen by the artists or pushed by the commercialization of female rappers, and whether they were participating in sexualized images of black women or pointing out the ironies, continues. Some feel that their unapologetic talk about sex, including their own preferences, and *their* choice to appear seminaked during public appearances are deliberate attempts to control the stereotypes of black women as objects for only masculine enjoyment (Peoples 25). What remains undisputed, however, is their popularity and ability to sell albums.

Getting her start with the Junior M.A.F.I.A., a group produced by Notorious B.I.G., Lil' Kim soon went solo, and her debut album, *Hard Core* (1996), lived up to the sexual suggestiveness of its title with singles like "Not Tonight":

> The moral of the story is this
> You ain't lickin' this, you ain't stickin' this

The reception of Lil' Kim's work was mixed: some found her entrance onto the male-dominated genre as a female artist from Brooklyn, New York, a bold new step for female rappers. Others found her explicit lyrics and scanty outfits further confirmation of the latent misogynist tendencies within hip hop culture.

Though Foxy Brown and Lil' Kim are often compared for their sexual explicitness in music and raunchy taste in dress and videos, Foxy is often known for her taste in high-fashion labels: "Cars and diamond rings, and nice braids, flaunt it / The Gucci boots with the G's on it." She also refers to luxury brands or luxury living commonly seen in the videos of male artists such as 50 Cent or Jay-Z.

The trend of sexually explicit female MCs continued, including Khia (aka Khia Chambers) and Trina (aka Katrina Laverne Taylor). Khia's "My Neck, My Back" from her debut album *Thug Misses* (2002) included direct instructions as to how she could be pleased: "So lick it now lick it good." Many were concerned that these women were being manipulated by the recording industry or by more established male producers as often their songs were produced or written by prominent men in the hip hop industry (Ogbar, "Hip Hop Revolution" 86). Their dress, lyrics, and videos borrowed from the male rapper tradition of bragging about sexual exploits and warnings not to mess with them. The popularity of both women was seen with their inclusion on the covers of popular industry magazines in addition to their record sales. With the advent of such artists, a debate began about the necessity of sexuality and violence to commercial success for male and female artists.

The interpretation of Foxy Brown and Lil' Kim was not entirely one sided. Critics pointed to the clear double standards in expectations for men and women addressed in their lyrics. In her song "My Life," for example, Foxy Brown wonders why for the same behavior a man with many women is considered a "mack" but a woman with many men a "whore" or why men are allowed to be rude while women are deemed bitches:

> Spit in faces, I never seem falsely accused
> While some say it's rude

The brashness and willingness at various points in Foxy Brown's music to talk about her own sexuality is reminiscent of the bravado previously expressed as a privilege of male rappers.

Other artists would come along in what some refer to as the third wave of female rappers in the vein of Queen Latifah and Salt-N-Pepa (Sharpley-Whiting xvii). They would continue to demonstrate a departure from the assumption that female artists did not need to be taken seriously with their volume in sales and awards. In 1999, for example, at the 41st Grammy Awards, a young woman named Lauryn Hill won five Grammys, the most ever by a woman at that time, for her debut solo album, *The Miseducation of Lauryn Hill* (1998). Awards included Best New Artist, Best R&B Song, and Best Female R&B Vocal Performance for the song "Doo Wop (That Thing)," Best R&B Album, and Album of the Year (Ogbar, "Hip Hop Revolution" 92). The album sold more than 200,000 copies in the first week (Price 156). In the lyrics for "Doo Wop (That Thing)," Hill calls women to a higher standard than that they have come to expect from men who use them sexually and then toss them aside:

> Girlfriend, let me break it down for you again
> You know I only say it 'cause I'm truly genuine

The smooth tone of her vocals and the power in her message ensured both critical and commercial success. As Theo Martins, rapper from Providence, Rhode Island, explains, Lauryn's success showed hip hop's ability to celebrate male and female artists:

Hip hop is about being creative, passionate, fresh and most of all yourself so it's great to see both men and women creatively expressing themselves within the artistic field. One of my favorite all time artists is Lauryn Hill so it's great that she can influence someone like myself to be progressive in the Arts. (Martins)

Martins points to Hill has an example of someone who does not follow the commercialization of hip hop in her lyrics with obscene language or images in her music.

Yet Hill's success was not without challenges: Her own image as an artist underwent transitions during this period as she shed the somewhat masculine clothing of hip hop culture characteristic of her style during her days with the group the Fugees for a sleeker look after her international success. Appearing on the cover of *Time* magazine that same year, under the title "Hip Hop Nation," Hill came to personify a culture that had clearly come far from its roots as an underground subculture (Heath 849). The glamorized Lauryn Hill who graced the covers of women's magazines had the signature beauty markers of popular culture: straightened hair, tight clothing, and precise make-up. Hill was slightly unprepared for all the media attention and retreated from public life for a short time, reappearing several years later in the vein of her original style (Perry 183). Despite her explosive debut success, Hill has not been able to replicate that response in the ensuing years—a fact that some see as an example of the challenges still facing female recording artists to establish and control their own careers beyond the initial novelty of their arrival on the musical scene (Hobson and Bartlow 5).

By 1999, Eve (Eve Jihan Jeffers), a female rapper backed by the male group the Ruff Ryders, used hip hop to address social issues such as domestic violence and other abusive behavior towards women. She was the first female MC to debut at number one with *Let There Be Eve . . . Ruff Ryders' First Lady* (1999) (Huntington 87). Perhaps even more frankly than Salt-N-Pepa's often feel-good groove, Eve's voice was one of unapologetic self-interest and power. Her song "Love is Blind" brings to the forefront issues related to domestic violence and empowering women to stand up against abuse as she tells the story of a friend killed by an abusive boyfriend. Eve creates a female-empowering anthem which calls attention to solidarity between women. She is not upset because someone is abusing her but because she is forced to watch as her friend is abused. Her hatred spills out against the male perpetrator:

> I don't even know you and I want you dead
> Don't know the facts but I saw the blood pour from her head

As the MC, she becomes the living witness to the friend's tragedy, and her lyrics are the tribute that the deceased woman is unlikely to receive from the community or her abusive partner. Eve is another artist like Queen Latifah who has made the transition from rapper to television actress, with the eponymous show *Eve*, which aired three seasons from 2003 to 2006. She has since guest starred in a variety of other sitcoms, including most recently *Glee*, and plays a self-confident, outspoken woman in most of her roles, including those in feature-length films such as *Barbershop* and *Beauty Shop*.

Another trailblazer, with her start as a writer for other artists, Missy "Misdemeanor" Elliott (aka Melissa Arnette Elliott) would become the reigning female rapper (Hemphill 390) and outsold many of her male counterparts. Her debut album, *Supa Dupa Fly* (1997), with hits like "The Rain," established her as a platinum-selling artist. At first, her style was both playful and witty with the emphasis on complex lyrics; she maintained a fine line between the socially aware music of Lauryn Hill and the sexual explicitness of Foxy Brown or Lil' Kim (Price 171). What followed were a string of commercially successful albums including *Da Real World* (1999) and *Miss E ... So Addictive* (2001), which included the popular club hit "Get Your Freak On" in which Elliott challenged others to take her on in the style of old school MC battles:

> Me and Timbaland been hot since twenty years ago
> What da dilly yo, now what da dilly yo

The reference to her work with Timbaland, who also rose to be one of hip hop's most important producers, is a testament to her lasting power in an industry plagued by one-hit wonders such as M.C. Hammer and Vanilla Ice. Elliot's "I'ma Bitch" gives voice to a fierce feminine persona that is here to stay on the music scene (Pough 101).

Not that all these achievements were made by women exclusively without the support of their male counterparts. Many of the most successful tracks recorded by these women were collaborations with male artists, proving that they could work together on equal footing. Missy Elliott's work with popular producer Timbaland and Lauryn Hill's recordings with Pras (aka Samuel Prakazrel Michel) and Wyclef Jean in the Fugees are examples of musical collaborations of

Female rapper Missy Elliott. (AP Photo/Fritz Kok/Handout.)

a strong female artist working closely together with popular male musicians that proved commercially and artistically successful (Emerson 129).

Newcomers to the scene are also taking on these messages of empowerment, activism, and presence. For example, young female Egyptian American rapper Mutamassik (aka Giulia Lolli) bends the musical genre to talk about politics, nature, and current events from her perspective as an Arab American. She was also a DJ and producer before committing to producing her own material, thus demonstrating the continued trend that those involved in hip hop culture tend to participate in more than one of its elements. Mutamassik's blog and YouTube videos show a woman who is not afraid to speak her mind, challenge the status quo, and present a positive image of women in the rap industry.

From the early days of "Rapper's Delight," produced by Sylvia Robinson, to female artists such as Salt-N-Pepa, Eve, and Missy

Elliott, women have had a strong presence in the hip hop music indus-try. They disrupt the limited representations of womanhood offered by rap music and in videos. Their work empowers women to tell their stories in their own voices, and their videos feature alternatives to the hypersexualized dancing performed by female dancers in songs by male rappers.

Conclusion

The grassroots outpouring of first- and second-generation immigrant teenagers in one of America's most economically depressed cities has developed into an internationally marketed consumer culture with diverse elements including dance, speech, film, television, fashion, and music reaching as far away as Japan, Tanzania, Senegal, Cuba, Great Britain, and New Zealand. The early days of hip hop tend to be written or looked back upon with nostalgia as a time when an MC was as likely to be a b-boy or graffiti artist as a multimillionaire and when the number of dancers at the party evaluated a DJ or MC by dancing to the music instead of buying an album. The spirit that created hip hop—disenfranchised youth creating their own platform to express dissatisfaction with social, economic, and political marginalization—has spread to teenagers on border reservations looking to express themselves in productive ways; not surprisingly, they turned to breaking for a sense of identity within the dominant culture (Deyhle 112). Other youth populations around the world, including rappers in Palestine, use hip hop to talk about abuse at the hands of the police, or government-supported racism, in ways reminiscent of N.W.A. or early hip hop artists, albeit in a new context (Maira 183).

The documentary film *Slingshot Hip Hop* follows the lives of young rappers in Gaza, the West Bank, and Israel as they use hip hop to address the sociopolitical reality of life in one of the world's most notorious conflict zones. Jackie Reem Salloum, director of the film, highlights how hip hop allowed these artists to use pop culture to challenge the stereotypes of Arabs. Hip hop in this setting is an intersection between pop culture and politics. Palestinian rappers like DAM showcase how rap can be a popular form of expression used by people around the world. Through their lyrics they educated youth about their history, identity, and culture. In many ways the story of DAM's work in Palestine is similar to that of the early days of hip hop when youth were on the streets with few productive choices for how to spend their time. DAM has created workshops for the kids to provide somewhere to go that takes them off the street and thereby show rap as a vibrant force in the ghetto. For a people that is divided by geopolitics, walls, and checkpoints, hip hop has helped connect people in their own country. Salloum is clear that Palestinian hip hop is not only positive for males but for females as well since there is no negative imagery in the lyrics or music videos. Chicago-based rapper Wundur reminds us that neither gender, nor race, nor nationality can determine how successful a rapper will be. It's down to the person's connection to the art form of rap itself: "To me a good MC is somebody that can present what he's saying in an understandable way, in a rhythmic way, in a stylish way, and stay on point with it" (Harkness).

Break dancing continues to entertain audiences around the world as a crossover medium while also establishing a growing respect and

Princess Anne watches break dancing at the Para Los Ninos family center in Los Angeles. (AP Photo/Doug Pizac.)

appreciation for breaking as an art form. The all-male German group the Flying Steps recently had a sold-out series of performances in Berlin, Germany, titled "Red Bull Flying Bach," in which their routines were choreographed to Johan Sebastian Bach's "Well-Tempered Clavier," a classical arrangement featuring keyboard solos that are between two and four minutes in length—the right amount of time for a breaking routine. Christopher Hagel, the music director of the show, comments on how the dancing emphasized the music: "What was interesting for me was to show visually, through the dancers, the structure of Bach fugues" (Williams). The b-boys were accompanied by a female, classically trained dancer, and the show's run time—70 minutes—attests to the ability of the unlikely combination of classical music and urban dancers to entertain a modern audience. The Flying Steps have won numerous dance contests, including the Battle of the Year, and are one of the most well-known b-boy groups performing today. Other fusions of hip hop include swing hop, which is a combination of hip hop dance and swing dance movements. The two elements have been combined to enhance the acrobatic effects of both. The dance style was featured prominently in the movie musical *Idewild* (2006) featuring music and acting by the hip hop group Outkast.

Nowadays, with the aid of YouTube videos and downloadable videos on the Internet, the aspiring b-boy or b-girl has ready access to hours of footage to perfect those crucial moves. Whereas in the past someone may have learned by watching live performances or from other members of a crew, an individual can rewind sequences from a break dancing movie from the privacy of his or her home. Hip hop dance as aerobic exercise has also become popular as well in video format for those who want the energetic movements to help burn calories. The average neighborhood dance studio also offers some form of breaking or hip hop classes to everyone from young children wanting variety in their after-school classes to athletes trying to increase their flexibility. There are online forums such as bboy.org which allow for a virtual community of b-boys and b-girls sharing tutorials on how to perform certain moves, news of upcoming battles, advice, tips, and videos for breakers at various levels. What has not changed are the long hours of practice required for a dancer to perfect techniques before dancing in front of other people.

The commercialization of hip hop has been one of the largest contentions between the "old school" artists and those who are selling records and concert tickets today. The divisions in the industry, some argue, have been fabricated or promoted by media hype—the East Coast versus West Coast "beef" or competition between rappers on the two coasts—but one cannot argue that their presence is pop culture flash in the pan compared to those artists who have proven their lasting power. Some commonly sum up the current situation regarding the ways the hip hop and rap are linked together: Hip hop is the culture, and rap is the music that developed out of that culture. Yet in the underground scene, and from the concert stages of artists like Queen Latifah or Jay-Z, there is the idea that rappers must do what they do out of love for the genre, not just the money. Again and again among the archival interviews for the documentary *I Am Hip Hop*, the interviewer hears rappers talk about having passion for what they do as a key element of successful rap:

> Kid Static: Everyone who comes out is like I'm the best rapper alive. And that's so subjective. You tell enough people you're the best rapper alive, yeah, they'll start to believe it. But I just wanna be respected for my craft. And just a love of hip hop. A love of what you're doing. You can use it as a business if you want to—people find different ways to make money. But I feel like the people who honestly love it, those are the people who it comes through. You can tell.
> KSOG: To be honest with you, man, it's all about your heart. It's all about you being real with what you do, loving your craft. (Harkness)

Now a multibillion-dollar industry, hip hop has outlasted the critics who thought it was a flash fad in the 1990s and those who wished it would fade away along with its images of nonstop partying or its socially conscious messages about inner city life. An industry at times plagued by considerable issues, including sexism and the glorification of violence in rap music, hip hop has both supporters and detractors from every segment of society: scholars at universities, youth in cities and suburbs, community activists—nearly everyone has heard about hip hop, and even more people have opinions about its relevance or appropriateness.

Women are present in modern day hip hop, elbowing to the center of the dance circle as b-girls, occupying the center of the stage as MCs, and bringing their unique messages into the industry and proving that they also can also break records in sales and performances. Yet debates within the hip hop community surround whether hip hop is really here to stay or whether it has "died," as famously stated by the rapper Nas (though he did say later that it still has a heartbeat).

Yet there is a sense of optimism among those who are engaged with hip hop culture at the grassroots level, or what others refer to as the underground. The documentary film *I Am Hip Hop: The Chicago Hip Hop Documentary* showcases the talent of MCs in urban settings who are far from the commercial deals of Jay-Z or Eminem and asks them a series of questions about hip hop culture, the language used in rap music, and the scene in Chicago in particular. Throughout the film, male and female rappers attest to their passion for hip hop, not just as an activity but as a lifestyle. When asked where they hoped to be in five years, most of the more than 20 interviewees respond that they would like to continue rapping and making a modest—not multibillion-dollar—living.

The title of the film, director Goeff Harkness explains, came from the repeated answer by interviewees when they were asked to define hip hop. "I am hip hop" is the answer that came back consistently (Harkness, interview). He comments that while the focus of the film was on the music, rap in particular, during the filming of the various artists, there were often other elements of hip hop present. People would be break dancing or rapping against a back drop of graffiti; as in the early days with DJ Kool Herc and Afrika Bambaataa, many of the rappers were introduced into hip hop culture by one of the other elements—graffiti, breaking, or DJing—and then discovered an interest in rap.

Marcyliena Morgan's study of rappers in the LA underground finds similar reactions among the aspiring rappers. They are still engaged in live battles in the communities in which they live; they are battling for respect, titles, and identity against others of their community. Many share the feeling that hip hop is alive and will continue to be so as long as people are involved in the underground scene. The grassroots origins of hip hop are what appeal to youth around the world today. As b-boy Smily (aka Danny Dibble) says:

> I believe that the underground movements that have evolved around djing, breaking, graffiti, and rapping, are what will drive the culture in the future. As the quality of mainstream rap goes down, people will naturally move back to where the culture started, the underground; the streets. Recently I have attended some local rap battles, and I think with

the death of mainstream hip hop, the underground battle scene will keep the art alive, similar to what happened with breaking. The sooner hip hopers realize that hip hop is not a business, it is an art medium, a culture and a way of expressing yourself, the sooner hip hop will achieve its true form. (Dibble)

What is undisputed is that no one could have predicted the trajectory of the earliest DJs and their improvised spinning, scratching, and cutting at block parties to the development of the MC who would dominate the music as a type of modern-day rebel, talking about social issues that affected the margins of society. Perhaps this is what is so mesmerizing about hip hop as a phenomenon; the energy, spontaneity,

Shamgod Geddi, member of the Breeze Team hip hop dance group. (AP Photo/ Michael Dwyer.)

and creativity that went into its inception is still keeping the beat going nearly 35 years later in both familiar and unexpected places.

Hip hop is an example of consumerism promoted by merchandise and yet also exists as a subversive street culture (Hobson and Bartlow 1). Johnny Lee of *Planet B-boy* hopes hip hop will continue to gain participants and credibility in the entertainment industry: "Hip-hop tends to get a bad reputation. I think the next step for b-boying would be to become more like the X Games here in America and start to be more accepted as a sport and competition" (Lee). But for people like b-boy Y-ray (aka Wairhe Napoleon) even traditional b-boy elements like battles still need to make the global rounds: "let them also try to bring battles to other continents which haven't heard much of b-boying such as African (Nigeria, Madagascar and Sudan), lets join hands together to make hip hop great and widespread cuz a tree cannot make a forest" (Napoleon).

Many have been looking beyond the now familiar arena of hip hop to the broader aspects of urban dance by further developing the power of b-boying to also incorporate other types of movement, including "clowning," a dance form developed by Tommy the Clown (aka Thomas Johnson) in the early 1990s to entertain children at birthdays and eventually high-profile celebrities. The "hip hop clown" was created almost by accident when Tommy appeared at a birthday party for a coworker's child dressed as a clown. His interactive dance style and use of upbeat, current music got the children dancing, as well as gave him an idea. Tommy the Clown went on to offer workshops training inner city kids in clowning, which came to refer to a mix of hip hop and playful clownish movements with dancers decked out in full clown makeup and clothing. The trend of hip hop clowns and their performances spread from one neighborhood to another. The movie documentary movie *Rize* (2007) showcases the emergence of clowning and krumping as social forces in the city of Los Angles. The dancers are agile and fast, popping various body parts, making swift spins, sometimes touching other dancers, and using their body weight to accomplish certain moves. This is in contrast to break dancing, where the lone dancer usually performs against a member of another crew, rarely or never touching.

Krumping is an aggressive form of street dance performed in an upright position rather than on the floor as with breaking. The fast movements of this dance style are often infused with anger by the performers. Krumping also has-inner city roots and was created by mentees of Tommy of the Clown. The film *Shake City 101* (2003) follows two krumping groups through the streets of LA until the final dance battle. The culture of krumping is similar to break dancing as dancers face off in crews and battle for titles as well as have nickname for their dancing alter egos. As with breaking, many point to the African roots of krumping, as many of the hip and pelvic movements are similar to the dances performed by slaves on plantations (Henry 124). Krump movements have been featured in popular hip hop videos including songs by Missy Elliot, Christina Aguilera, and others. Both clowning and krumping are ways to escape gang culture and enhance one's creative skills.

Others are busy preserving the historic sites and artifacts of hip hop's origins. In September 2010, the mortgage to the building on 1520 Sedgewick Avenue was acquired by the Workforce Housing Advisors in an effort to rehabilitate the building where DJ Kool Herc first spun the beats at parties held in the building's community room that are now hip hop legend (Dolnick A23). This move on the part of tenants, housing advocates, and city agencies to keep a historic building from further deterioration shows a reversal of the splitting up of the Bronx during the 1970s and the demolition of buildings to introduce the subway, and an effort to preserve some of the history and sense of place of the early days of DJing and break dancing. Efforts to preserve history in the neighborhoods where hip hop was created include the Hollis Hip Hop Museum and Hollis Famous Burgers. In the modest burger joint in Hollis, Queens, home to the group Run-DMC customers can enjoy mini burgers while seeing gold and platinum records by the neighborhood's most famous group (Kilgannon A23). Even universities are paying attention to the impact and influence of hip hop culture. The most prestigious names in academia, including Stanford, Harvard, Berkeley, Duke, and the University of Pennsylvania, offer courses on hip hop culture, theory, and music. This trend is not limited to American universities but also reaches international ones such as the University of London's Education Institute, which featured a unit on Rap/Poetry to help engage students with the work of classic poets such as William Wordsworth via the lyrics of Nas and Eminem. The rhythmic elements of rap music are also being used to help children memorize their multiplication tables and other important information in a fun and interactive way as shown by teacher Harriett Ball in the documentary on public school education *Waiting for Superman*. Repeated rhythmic recitation of lines in musical form is also being used by those who wish to memorize the entire Qur'an.

From graffiti in Australia to b-girl competitions in Germany, the founding elements of hip hop culture are thriving around the world wherever there are teenagers or disenfranchised youth; hip hop continues as a force to empower youth to express their identities in sociopolitical awareness. Hip hop culture remains accessible to those who want to experiment with its foundational elements regardless of their nationality, gender, or class. Even within America, the power of hip hop as a culture is still evident. Chicago-based Moneybagz explains it this way: "So hip hop is a way of life. We influence the way people walk, the way people dress, the things that come out of politicians and religious figures mouths. These days, we so heavy in the game, preachers have to incorporate slang in church. Real talk. So, that's hip hop. Hip hop is a total way of life. It's a real movement. It's not just rap. That's only one" (Harkness). Whether it's a b-boy in South Korea competing in a battle to establish his reputation in one of the most militarized zones in the world or the lyrics of a Palestinian rapper trying to raise the awareness of humanitarian issues in the Gaza strip, the vehicle of hip hop is now being used to express the hopes, aspirations, and goals of yet another multicultural generation.

Glossary

b-boy (also *break boy*).   Term referring to male dancers who would dance to the break beats at parties, eventually performing in groups; sometimes used interchangeably to refer to male and female dancers.

b-girl.   The female equivalent of a b-boy.

battle.   Any competition related to graffiti writing, DJing, MCing, or breaking or break dancing where two or more competitors vie for a title.

bombing (also *bombin'*).   Term used by graffiti writers to refer to covering a large area.

breaking (also *break dancing*).   Form of improvised dance involving spins and flips.

burning.   Getting the best of your competitor whether in dancing, graffiti writing, DJing, or MCing.

crews.   Groups of b-boys and b-girls, often organized by neighborhood or geographic location, to gain entrance into which one often had to perform competitively.

dj.   Person at parties spinning records, known in the 1970s for putting together beats from various records.

graffiti.   Style of street art made popular on subway cars in the 1970s, done with spray paint or markers.

freeze.   Holding a pose in a break dancing routine.

hip hop generation.   Term used to refer to the youth between 1965 and 1984.

mc (also *emcee, master of ceremonies*).   Person invited by a DJ to keep the crowd moving to the music with improvised lyrics.

old school.   Refers to the period of time before the commercialization of hip hop in the mainstream media, generally the 1970s.

rapper.   Commercialized name for an MC.

tags (tagging, taggers).   One's graffiti nickname written on public surfaces.

Discography

Coolio, "Fantastic Voyage," *It Takes a Thief*, Tommy Boy (1994).

DJ Jazzy Jeff and the Fresh Prince, "Girls Ain't Nothing but Trouble," *Rock the House*, Jive (1987).

DJ Jazzy Jeff and the Fresh Prince, "Parents Just Don't Understand," *He's the DJ, I'm the Rapper*, Jive (1988).

Grandmaster Flash and the Furious Five, "The Message," Sugar Hill (1982).

MC Lyte, "Ruffneck," Atlantic (1991).

Nate Dogg (featuring Warren G), "Regulators," *Regulate G-Funk Era*, Def Jam (1994).

Salt-N-Pepa, "Push It," *Hot, Cool & Vicious*, Next Plateau Records (1988).

Salt-N-Pepa, "Let's Talk about Sex," *Blacks' Magic*, Next Plateau Records (1991).

Salt-N-Pepa, "Whatta Man." *Very Necessary*, Next Plateau Records (1993).

Salt-N-Pepa (featuring En Vogue), "Shoop," *Very Necessary*, Next Plateau Records (1993).

Sugar Hill Gang, "Rapper's Delight," Sugar Hill (1979).

Queen Latifah (featuring Monie Love), "Ladies First," *All Hail the Queen*, Tommy Boy (1989).

Queen Latifah, "U.N.I.T.Y." *Black Reign*, Motown (1993).

Bibliography

Adams, Terri M., and Douglas B. Fuller. "The Words Have Changed But the Ideology Remains the Same: Misogynistic Lyrics in Pop Music." *Journal of Black Studies* 36.6 (2006): 938–57.

Alder, Barbara. Email interview. 22 Aug 2010.

Aldridge, Derrick P. "From Civil Rights to Hip Hop: Towards a Nexus of Ideas." *The Journal of African American History* 90.3, The History of Hip Hop (Summer, 2005): 226–52.

Alim, H. Samy. "Hip Hop Global Hood: Youth's Global Culture." *Muslim Networks: From Hajj to Hip Hop.* Ed. Miriam Cooke and Bruce B. Lawrence. Durham: University of North Carolina Press, 2005. 268–73.

Als, Hilton, and Darryl A. Turner. *White Noise: The Eminem Collection.* New York: De Capo Press, 20030.

Antonio, Marko. Interview with Author. 14 Oct 2010.

Apell, Glenn, and David Hemphill. *American Popular Music: A Multicultural History.* Florence, Kentucky: Thomson Wadsworth, 2006.

Asante, M. K. Jr. *It's Bigger than Hip Hop: The Rise of the Post Hip Hop Nation.* New York: St. Martin's Griffin, 2009.

Banes, Sally. *Writing Dancing in the Age of Postmodernism.* Middletown, CT: Wesleyan University Press, 1994.

Black Dot. *Hip Hop Decoded: From Its Ancient Origin to Its Modern Day Matrix.* New York: Mome, 2005.

Boyd, Todd. *The New N.H.N.I.C: The Death of Civil Rights and the Reign of Hip Hop.* New York: New York University Press, 2003.

Boyer, Bryan. Email interview. 19 Aug 2010.

Bradley, Adam. *Book of Rhymes: The Poetics of Hip Hop.* Tennessee: Basic Civitas Books, 2009.

Brown, Ethan. *Queens Reigns Supreme: Fat Cat, 50 Cent, and the Rise of the Hip Hop Hustler.* New York: Knopf, 2005.

Burton, Michael. Email interview. 21 Aug 2010.

Carpenter, Faedra Chatard. "An Interview with Gwendolyn D. Pough." *Callaloo* 29.3 (Summer 2006): 808–814.

Castleman, Craig. *Getting Up: Subway Graffiti in New York*. Cambridge, MA: The MIT Press, 1984.

Chang, Jeff. *Can't Stop Won't Stop: A History of the Hip Hop Generation*. New York: Picador, 2005.

Chang, Juliana. "Keeping It Real: Interpreting Hip Hop." *College English* 68.5 (May 2006): 545–54.

Cheney, Charise L. *Brothers Got to Work It Out: Sexual Politics in the Golden Age of Rap Nationalism*. New York: New York University Press, 2005.

Cobb, William Jelani. *To the Break of Dawn: A Freestyle on the Hip Hop Aesthetic*. New York: New York University Press, 2007.

Collins, Michael. "Biggie Envy and the Gangsta Sublime." *Callaloo* 29.3 (Summer 2006): 911–38.

Collins, Patricia Hill. *From Black Power to Hip Hop: Racism, Nationalism, and Feminism*. Philadelphia, PA: Temple University Press, 2006.

Condry, Ian. "Yellow B-Boys, Black Culture, and Hip-Hop in Japan: Toward a Transnational Cultural Politics of Race." *Positions: East Asia Cultures Critique* 15.3 (Winter 2007): 637–71.

Cooper, Martha, and Henry Chalfant. *Subway Art: 25th Anniversary Edition*. San Francisco: First Chronicle Books, 2009.

Crossley, Scott. "Metaphorical Conceptions in Hip Hop Music." *African American Review* 39.4 (Winter 2005): 501–512.

Deyhle, Donna. "Break Dancing and Breaking Out: Anglos, Utes, and Navajos in a Border Reservation High School." *Anthropology and Education Quarterly* 17.2 (June 1986): 111–27.

Dibble, Danny. Email interview. 27 Aug 2010.

Dimitriadis, Greg. "Hip Hop: From Live Performance to Mediated Narrative." *Popular Music* 15.2 (1996): 179–94.

Dolnick, Sam. "Hope for a Bronx Tower of Hip Hop Love." *The New York Times* 7 Sep. 2010: A23.

Dyson, Michael E. *Reflecting Black: African-American Cultural Criticism*. Minneapolis: University of Minnesota Press, 1993.

Dyson, Michael E., and Sohail Daulatzai. *Born to Use the Mics: Reading Nas' Illmatic*. Tennessee: Basic Civitas Book, 2009.

Emerson, Rana. "'WHERE MY GIRLS AT?': Negotiating Black Womanhood in Music Videos." *Gender and Society* 16.1 (2002): 115–35.

Engel, Lis. "Body Poetics of Hip Hop Dance Styles in Copenhagen." *Dance Chronicle* 24.3 (2001): 351–72.

Fine, Elizabeth Calvert. *Soul Stepping: African American Step Shows*. Champaign: University of Illinois, 2003.

Fisher, Curtis (Grandmaster Caz). Foreword. *Hip Hop Decoded*. Eds. The Black Dot (Latonia Almeyda-Bowser, Sylvon Wright and James Top). New York: Mome, xv–xvi.

Fitzgerald, Tamsin. *Hip Hop and Urban Dance*. Chicago, IL: Heinemann Library, 2009.

Fitzpatrick, Tracy. *Art and the Subway: New York Underground*. Rutgers, NJ: Rutgers University Press, 2009.

Flores, Juan. *From Bomba to Hip Hop*. New York: Columbia University Press, 2000.

FNV Newsletter. "An Interview with RSC President Crazy Legs." (July 2002). http://www.daveyd.com/fnvdirect.html.

Forman, Murray. *The Hood Comes First: Race, Space, and Place in Rap and Hip Hop.* Middletown, CT: Wesleyan University Press, 2002.

Forman, Murray, and Mark Anthony Neal. *That's the Joint!: The Hip Hop Studies Reader.* New York: Routledge, 2004.

Fricke, Jim, and Charlie Ahearn. *Yes Yes Y'All: The Experience Music Project Oral History of Hip Hop's First Decade.* Cambridge, MA: Decapa Press, 2002.

Garcia, Ana (Rockafella). "Herstory." *We B*Girlz Festival Magazine* (2008): 58–59.

Gladney, Marvin J. "The Black Arts Movement and Hip Hop." *African American Review* 29.2, Special Issue on The Music (1995): 291–301.

Grant, Kyra. *Games Black Girls Play: Learning the Ropes from Double Dutch to Hip Hop.* New York: New York University Press, 2006.

Green, Jarius, and David Brammell. *Hip Hop Handbook Vol. 1. Breakdance.* Olympia, WA: Street Style Publications, 2003.

Greenwald, Jeff. "Hip-Hop Drumming: The Rhyme May Define, But the Groove Makes You Move." *Black Music Journal* 22.2 (Autumn 2002): 259–71.

Gültekin, Ayhan Adem. Email interview. 21 Aug 2010.

Guzman-Sanchez, Thomas. "There Is No Such Thing as Breakdance." http://www.dancemaster.com/nobkdn.html#Anchor-Letter. Retrieved September 15, 2010.

Hagar, Steven. *Hip Hop: The Illustrated History of Break Dancing, Rap Music, and Graffiti.* New York: St. Martin's Press, 1984.

Hamilton, Carla Stalling. *Hip Hop Dance: Meanings and Messages.* Jefferson, NC: McFarland and Company, 2007.

Harkness, Geoff. Interview with Author. 14 Sept 2010.

Harkness, Geoff. *Situational Authenticity in Chicago's Hip-Hop Underground.* Unpublished Dissertation. Northwestern University. 2010.

Heath, Scott. "True Heads: Historicizing the Hip Hop 'Nation' in Context." *Callaloo* 29.3 (Summer 2006): 846–66.

Heath, Scott. "Hip Hop Now: An Introduction." *Callaloo* 29.3, Hip-Hop Music and Culture (Summer, 2006) 714–16.

Henning, Schaefer. Interview with Author. 4 Nov 2010.

Henry, Audrey Taylor. *The Sound of Applause.* Pennsylvania: Red Letter Press, 2009.

Hess, Mickey. *Icons of Hip Hop: An Encyclopedia of the Movement, Music, and Culture,* Vol 1. Westport, CT: Greenwood Press, 2007.

Hobson, Janell, and R. Dianne Bartlow. "Introduction: Representin': Women, Hip-hop, and Popular Music." *Meridians: Feminism, Race, Transnationalism* 8.2. (2008): 1–14.

Holman, Michael. "Breaking: The History." *That's the Joint: Hip Hop Studies Reader.* Eds. Murray Forman and Mark Anthony Neal. New York: Routledge, 2004. 34–45.

Huntington, Stalling Carla. *Hip Hop Dance: Meanings and Messages.* NC: McFarland, 2007.

Jooda. Interview with Author. 26 Aug 2010.

Keyes, Cheryl L. *Rap Music and Street Consciousness: Music in American Life.* Champaign: University of Illinois Press, 2004.

Kilgannon, Corey. "Putting Together a Hamburger, a Neighborhood, and Hip-Hop." *The New York Times* 20 Feb. 2009: A23.

Kitwana, Bakari. *Why White Kids Love Hip Hop: Wanksters, Wiggars, Wannabes and the New Reality of Race in America.* New York: Basic Civitas Books, 2006.

LaBennett, Oneka. "Histories and Herstories from the Bronx: Excavating Hidden Hip Hop Narratives." *AfroAmericans in New York Life and History* 33.2 (2009): 109–131.

LaBoskey, Sara. "Getting Off: Portrayals of Masculinity in Hip Hop Dance in Film." *Dance Research Journal* 33.2, Social and Pop Dance (Winter 2001): 112–20.

Lacey, Brenda Washington. *Feet Don't Fail Me Now: Devastating Divas in Drill and Step*. Bloomington, IN: AuthorHouse, 2007.

Lee, Johnny. Email interview. 31 Aug. 2010.

Leland, John. *Hip: The History*. New York: Harper Collins, 2004.

Loayza, Angel. Interview with Author. 5 Nov 2010.

Maira, Sunaina. "'We Ain't Missing': Palestinian Hip Hop—A Translational Youth Movement." *The New Centennial Review* 8.2 (Fall 2008): 61–192.

Mapue, Allen Maverick G. Email interview. 20 Aug. 2010.

Martins, Theo. Email interview. 20 Aug. 2010.

Martinez, Theresa A. "Popular Culture as Oppositional Culture: Rap as Resistance." *Sociological Perspectives* 40.2 (1997): 265–86.

Morgan, Joan. "Fly Girls, Bitches and Hoes: Notes of a Hip Hop Feminist." *Social Text* 45 (Winter 1995): 151–57.

Morgan, Marcyliena. *The Real Hip Hop: Battling for Knowledge, Power, and Respect in the LA Underground*. Durham, NC: Duke University Press, 2009.

Napoleon, Wairhe. Email interview. 20 Aug. 2010.

Nelson, George. *Hip Hop America*. New York: Penguin, 2005.

Ogbar, Jeffrey O. G. "Slouching toward Bork: The Culture Wars and Self Criticism in Hip Hop Music." *Journal of Black Studies* 30.2 (1999): 164–83.

Ogbar, Jeffrey O. G. *Hip Hop Revolution: The Culture and Politics of Rap*. Lawrence: University of Kansas, 2007.

Peoples, Whitney A. "Under Construction: Identifying Foundations of Hip-Hop Feminism and Exploring Bridges between Black Second-Wave and Hip-Hop Feminisms." *Meridians: Feminism, Race, Transnationalism* 8.2. (2008): 19–52.

Perry, Imani. *Prophets of the Hood*. Durham, NC: Duke University Press, 2005.

Phillips, Layli, Kerri Reddick-Morgan, and Dionne Patricia Stephens. "Oppositional Consciousness within an Oppositional Realm: The Case of Feminism and Womanism in Rap and Hip Hop, 1976–2004." *The Journal of African American History* 90.3 (Summer 2005): 253–77.

Pough, Gwendolyn, D. *Check It While I Wreck It: Black Womanhood, Hip Hop Culture, and the Public*. Boston, MA: Northeastern UP, 2004.

Price, Emmett G. III. *Hip Hop Culture*. Santa Barbara, CA: ABC-CLIO, 2006.

Rahn, Janice. *Painting without Permission: Hip-Hop Graffiti Subculture*. Westport, CT: Bergin and Garvey, 2002.

Ramsey, Guthrie P., Jr. *Race and Music: Black Cultures from Bebop to Hip-Hop*. Berkley: University of California Press, 2003.

Reid-Brinkley, Shanara R. "The Essence of Res(ex)pectablity: Black Women's Negotiation of Black Femininity in Rap Music and Music Video." *Meridians: Feminism, Race, Transnationalism* 8.2 (2008): 236–60.

Riveria, Raquel. *New York Ricans from the Hip Hop Zone*. New York: Palgrave Macmillan, 2003.

Rose, Tricia. *Black Noise: Rap Music and Black Culture in Contemporary America*. Middletown, CT: Wesleyan University Press, 1994.

Rose, Tricia. *Hip Hop Wars: What We Talk about When We Talk about Hip Hop and Why It Matters*. New York: Basic Civitas Books, 2008.

Saddick, Annette J. "Rap's Unruly Body: The Postmodern Performance of Black Male Identity on the American Stage." *The Drama Review* 47.4 (Winter 2003): 110–27.

Saňák, Kamil. Email interview. 18 Aug. 2010.

Sanchez, Jasper. Email interview. 19 Aug. 2010.

Satoria, Stanley. Email interview. 22 Aug. 2010.

Schloss, Joseph Glenn. *Making Beats: The Art of Sample Based Hip Hop.* Middletown, CT: Wesleyan University Press, 2004.

Schloss, Joseph Glenn. *Foundation: B-boys, B-girls, and Hip Hop Culture.* Oxford, England: Oxford University Press, 2009.

Sharpley-Whiting, Denean T. *Pimps Up, Ho's Down: Hip Hop's Hold on Young Black Women.* New York: New York University Press, 2007.

Sherman, Sharon R. "Bombing, Breakin', and Gettin' Down: The Folk and Popular Culture of Hip-Hop." *Western Folklore* 43.4. (October 1984): 287–93.

Smith, William E. *Hip Hop as Performance and Ritual.* British Columbia, Canada: Trafford Publishing, 2006.

Starr, Larry, and Christopher Waterman. *American Popular Music: From Minstrelsy to MP3,* 2nd edition. New York: Oxford University Press: 2007.

Stephens, Vincent. "Pop Goes the Rapper: A Close Reading of Eminem's Genderphobia." *Popular Music.* 24.1 (2005): 21–36.

Tanz, Jason. *Other People's Property: A Shadow History of Hip Hop in White America.* New York: Bloomsbury, 2007.

Tokaji, András. "The Meeting of Sacred and Profane in New York's Music: Robert Moses, Lincoln Center, and Hip-Hop." *Journal of American Studies* 29.1 (1995): 97–103Wang, Oliver. *Classic Material: The Hip Hop Album Guide.* New York: ECW Press, 2003.

Watkins, S. Craig. *Hip Hop Matters: Politics, Pop Culture, and the Struggle for the Soul of the Movement.* Boston, MA: Beacon Press, 2006.

Wheeler, Elizabeth. "Most of My Heroes Don't Appear on No Stamps: The Dialogics of Rap Music." *Black Music Research Journal* 11.2 (Autumn 1991): 193–96.

Williams, Gisela. "In Berlin, Break Dancing to Bach." *The New York Times,* 22 Apr. 2010. http://intransit.blogs.nytimes.com/2010/04/22/in-berlin-break-dancing-to-bach/. Retrieved 17 Sept. 2010.

Wimsatt, William Upski. *Bomb the Suburbs: Graffiti, Race, Freight Hopping and the Search for Hip Hop's Moral Center.* New York: Soft Skull Press, 2001.

Index

About the Author

Mohanalakshmi Rajakumar is a writer, educator, and scholar of literature. She has a Ph.D. from the University of Florida and is interested in cultural studies, gender, and postcolonial theory. She has published short stories, academic articles, and travel essays in a variety of journals and literary magazines as well as an academic monograph. Rajakumar also reviews audio books for *Audiofile* magazine and regularly contributes to *Writers and Artists Yearbook* as a guest blogger.

Her first book, *Haram in the Harem* (2009), deals with the images of the female Muslim housewife in the writings of women from the Indian subcontinent and North Africa. She coedited *Qatari Voices* (2010), a volume of essays written by citizens of Qatar on issues important to their everyday lives.

Rajakumar is the creator and coeditor of the *Qatar Narratives* series, a Qatar-produced and -published anthology project which gives a platform to the experiences of residents and citizens living in Qatar and which is now in its third volume, *Dreesha: Glimpses of Qatar*, a collection of photo essays. More information about her work can be found on her website: www.mohanalakshmi.com.